Foucault, Marxism and Critique

FOUCAULT, MARXISM AND CRITIQUE

Barry Smart

Routledge & Kegan Paul
London, Boston, Melbourne and Henley

First published in 1983
by Routledge & Kegan Paul plc
39 Store Street, London WC1E 7DD,
9 Park Street, Boston, Mass. 02108, USA,
296 Beaconsfield Parade, Middle Park,
Melbourne, 3206, Australia, and
Broadway House, Newtown Road,
Henley-on-Thames, Oxon RG9 1EN
Printed in Great Britain by
Redwood Burn Ltd., Trowbridge, Wilts

British Library Cataloguing in Publication Data

Smart, Barry
Foucault, Marxism and critique.
1. Foucault, Michel
I. Title
194   B2430.F724

ISBN 0-7100-9533-3

For J.B.

The dialectical form of exposition is only correct when it knows its limits. (Marx)

Knowledge works as a tool of power. Hence it is plain that it increases with every increase of power. (Nietzsche)

CONTENTS

ACKNOWLEDGMENTS

I would like to thank the many people who have offered constructive comment and criticism at various stages of the development of the work that has gone into the manuscript. Discussions with groups of students and with colleagues at the University of Sheffield and Griffith University, Brisbane, have in particular been a source of both support and insight.

Most of all, however, I wish to express my thanks to Jeremy Agnew for his detailed comments and wise counsel, Russell Hogg for deferring his return to Australia until we had discussed the formative stages of the work in some detail, Carol Smart for companionship and encouragement, and Jo Burgin for her generosity, understanding and support.

Finally my gratitude to Thelma Kassell, Sylvia Parkin, Val Squire and Margaret Scarr for their speedy and conscientious typing of the manuscript.

INTRODUCTION

Although a series of complex and significant social, political, cultural and economic changes have occurred in the course of the twentieth century, we have continued to make sense of the present, of our society, social relationships, politics and culture in terms largely derived from the classical texts of sociology, political economy and philosophy, and nowhere has this been more in evidence than in the case of critical forms of analysis and theory, for which the classical texts of the Marxist tradition have constituted the appropriate and necessary point of reference. Notwithstanding observations on the possible significance of the emergence of a multiplicity of transformations in the form and structure of the advanced capitalist societies of the Western world, and the steady accumulation of a wealth of evidence and experience which indicates that the process of development of the societies of 'actually existing socialism' has assumed an unanticipated and increasingly undesirable form, critical analyses have continued to be articulated principally in Marxist terms. The world in which we live may have changed in many ways, but the concepts and modes of analysis in terms of which we have continued to make sense of the present have remained deeply rooted in nineteenth-century thought.

One possible explanation would be that this signifies nothing more than an appreciation of the continuing general relevance of Marxist analysis for an understanding of the formation, structure and development of contemporary societies. An implication of this would seem to be that the changes which have been identified in the advanced capitalist societies, for example in class structure, in levels and forms of politicisation - notably the apparent decline or disappearance of a 'radicalised' working class and emergence of 'non-class' political subject groups - and in the development of complex relations and technologies of power, are either relatively insignificant, constituting merely temporary interludes in a broader historical process, or are entirely explicable in terms of formulations derived from a Marxist analytical framework. Likewise, the manifest problems of the societies of 'actually existing socialism' may be interpreted as either the inevitable painful symptoms of a complex and difficult transitional phase in the development of socialism, as revealing difficulties which no theory could have possibly anticipated, or alternatively as evidence that such societies have lost their way, have failed to fulfil the promise of the revolution, in short as signifying a departure from the develop-

mental programme sketched out in the classical texts of the
Marxist tradition. Either way Marxist analysis is relatively
insulated from interrogation, the assumption of its general relevance unchallenged.

Another, possibly better explanation might be that there has
been no appropriate alternative to Marxism, that as far as the
construction of critical forms of theorising is concerned our
whole conceptual framework has necessarily been Marxist, we
have had no other vocabulary through which to articulate our
analyses without running the risk of giving hostage to the
Right. In consequence the identification of problems and limitations in Marxist theory and politics has elicited a somewhat
predictable response, namely a return to the classical texts of
the tradition to discover a solution.

The indications are that this state of affairs has begun to
change, that the processes of reinterpretation, reformulation,
and reconstruction of the concepts and analyses present in the
classical texts of the tradition have been virtually exhausted.
Therefore, although the assumption of the general relevance of
Marxist analysis has continued to receive a degree of endorsement, and predictable reassurances have continued to be
offered that 'the situation of crisis within which we live today
offers an opportunity to close the gap between Marxist theory
and working class struggle' (Callinicos, 1982, p. 225), it has
become increasingly evident that all is not well with socialist
theory and politics, in brief, that there exists what has been
described as a 'crisis of Marxism' (cf. Laclau and Mouffe, 1981).

Contributions to the debate on the crisis of Marxism have
varied considerably, as one might expect given the presence
within the Marxist tradition of significant differences in epistemology, methodology, and interpretation of the classical texts.
However, a common denominator has generally been present in
the form of a commitment to re-establish the authority of Marxist
theory and analysis and to prescribe the appropriate line(s)
along which socialist political strategy might develop. This
commitment has been honoured in various ways, but increasingly
through recourse to the work of Gramsci. In some instances,
where the past and present limits and limitations of Marxism
have been rigorously and quite conclusively delineated, there
would seem to be little scope for a subsequent process of
internal renewal, and it is in such contexts that particular non-
Marxist forms of theory and analysis have been identified as
the source of a potential advance.

The implication here is not that Marx(ism) is dead or that
historical materialism may be safely relegated to the museum of
the history of ideas, but rather that the cumulative effect of
the series of attempts to resolve the problems of Marxism by
reinterpreting the classical texts (e.g. Marx of the 'Economic
and Philosophic Manuscripts', Marx of the 'Grundrisse', or
of 'Capital'; the respective works of Lenin, Trotsky, Lukács,
and Gramsci, etc.) has been the precipitation of a residue of

comparable problems, albeit conceptualised at times in different terms, which testify to the necessary limits and inevitable limitations of Marxist analysis, and signify the necessity of deploying, in addition, other concepts and other modes of analysis in order to understand the present.

A history of Marxism reveals the irregular presence of a discriminating openness towards particular non-Marxist forms of analysis and inquiry, viz. the respective works of Freud and Weber; existential and phenomenological philosophy; and more recently feminist theory and analysis - all of which have had an impact on or within Marxist analysis. However, in each instance the tendency has been towards an incorporation of apparently compatible elements of 'alien' philosophies in order to further advance the construction of a more global and systematised Marxist theory. A contemporary example would be the constructive responses by some Marxists to the work of Foucault (cf. Lecourt, 1975; Poulantzas, 1978).

It is in this context, namely of a discussion of the critical problems of Marxism and associated debates and responses, that I have attempted to locate my commentary on the work of Foucault.

1 ON THE LIMITS AND LIMITATIONS OF MARXISM

From the beginning any examination of Marxism is likely to encounter and to promote controversy, for Marxism is a veritable cauldron of interpretations and schools of thought. There may have been only one 'biographical' Marx, but the literature abounds with conceptions of the 'total', 'early', 'mature', 'scientific' or 'humanist' Marx. In addition, there are a plethora of clearly differentiated Marxisms, although not quite, as one commentator would have it, 'almost as many Marxisms as there are Marxists' (Bobbio, 1979a, p. 193). However, underlying the cultural and epistemological differences manifested in the form of several national Marxisms (e.g. Austro-Marxism, English Marxism, etc.) and a variety of rigorously differentiated schools of Marxist thought (e.g. 'humanist' Marxism, 'structuralist' Marxism) there are specific common features, reference points and predicaments. My attention will be directed to these more general elements and conditions and will be focused in particular upon the contemporary diagnosis of a 'crisis of Marxism'.

This is not the first occasion on which the history of Marxism has been punctuated by the cry of 'crisis'; however, the contemporary reference has a qualitatively different significance, for it denotes that a decisive moment or a historic turning point has been reached. Whereas in the past statements about the problems associated with Marxist theory and politics may have emanated from opposing political forces, from those opposed to the Labour Movement, now discussion of the 'crisis of Marxism' encompasses Marxists, fellow-travellers and radical social theorists alike (cf. Anderson, 1976; Althusser, 1978a; Altvater and Kallscheuer, 1979). Although it is difficult to single out any one issue as the catalyst for the current concern, it is evident that an interrogation of the nature of socialism, of the possibility of an alternative social order, is at the heart of the crisis of Marxism. What seems to have taken place is a reassessment of the societies of 'actually existing socialism', and in place of the routine and heavily ritualised defence and expression of sympathetic understanding with the difficulties encountered by the Soviet Union and its Eastern European allies in their 'transitional phase' there has emerged a refreshingly critical reconsideration of the limitations of the societies of 'actually existing socialism' (cf. Berlinguer, 1982). Whereas the limitations might once have been explained away as temporary or transitional features of societies progressing along the path to communism, they are now considered to represent the development of a qualitatively different social order or to signify a termination of the transitional process (cf. Bahro, 1978).

The development of a more critical analytical orientation towards the societies of Eastern Europe and the corollary, namely a belated recognition that perhaps their development is incompatible with the promise of Marxist theory, has had two consequences. First, there has been increasing support for the observation that there no longer exists any model for socialism, that our knowledge extends only as far as that which is to be avoided, namely Soviet-style socialism. In turn this has precipitated the formulation of a series of questions concerning, on the one hand, the unrealised conception of socialism, in particular the possibility and desirability of its realisation, and, on the other hand, the reality of the societies of 'actually existing socialism', of how they came to develop in their present form and whether they constitute a realisation of Marxist theory, or are merely pathological forms or deviations. Marxism seems to have few, if any, satisfactory answers to these particular questions. A second and related consequence has been that Marxist theory itself has been critically examined and found to be both limited and deficient. To begin with, specific concepts and premises within Marxist theory have been identified as problematic, for example the premise of economic determination-in-the-final-instance, the conceptualisation of politics and power and the theorising of the relationship between structure, action and consciousness. Furthermore, the epistemological basis of Marxist analysis has become a matter of controversy. The scientific status of Marxism has itself become a critical issue of inquiry.

In this chapter I will being by briefly outlining the major characteristics of the contemporary crisis of Marxism in terms of a distinction between its theoretical and political dimensions. I will then proceed to examine each of these dimensions in more detail.

THE CRISIS OF MARXISM

An assumption of a positive and close relationship between theory and political practice has generally constituted a fundamental feature of Marxist analysis. It has frequently been stated that Marxist theory may be realised in practice, that the truth or validity of its knowledge may be confirmed or given by the objective results of social practice (cf. Kolakowski, 1971, p. 59; Mao, 1971, pp. 67-8). However, it also seems to have been the case that the appropriate moment for the realisation of theory has remained, with perhaps one or two controversial exceptions (e.g. the Russian Revolution), in a relatively indeterminate future. Hence, alongside an emphasis on social and political practice as some sort of 'mechanism of verification' we will also find that the question of the theory-practice relationship within Marxism has remained both ambiguous and problematical (cf. Anderson, 1976; Poulantzas, 1978), although a tendency to accord priority to the political dimension, to political practice, has remained a consistent feature of Marxist discourse.

Given the significance of formulations of the relationship between theory and political practice within Marxism it comes as no surprise that a series of events which took place in 1968 have been consistently identified as the locus of the emergence of the contemporary crisis of Marxism. In particular it is the events of May in France and the events known as the 'Prague Spring' in Czechoslovakia which have been located at the epicentre of the current crisis of Marxism. These events brought into focus once more a series of issues which have been the source of intermittent controversy throughout the history of Marxism. The events of the 'Prague Spring' and its aftermath served to draw attention once again to the reality of Eastern European socialism and forced Marxists to readdress a series of questions and problems to which there could be no easy answers. The events of 'May '68' in France and other forms of protest elsewhere in the West caused Marxists to reflect upon the continuing incompatibility of their theoretical 'expectations' with the pattern of development of Western capitalist societies. Both sets of events disrupted conventional forms of Marxist discourse and precipitated the process of re-examination, reformulation and reconceptualisation of which we have yet to hear the last. This is not the place to explore these events in detail, but it is necessary to make a few additional comments on the events of May '68, for they may be regarded as of some significance in the development of new forms of politics and new forms of analysis.

There are two observations to be made on the events of May '68. First, the forms of popular protest and political action involved mass movements of people. These movements seemed to emerge spontaneously. They were formed independently and outside of the conventional political institutions of opposition, namely the trade unions and the political parties of the Left. Finally they were informally or non-bureaucratically organised around quite specific struggles which could not be simply conceptualised as class struggles. The second observation which needs to be made is that the Communist Party in France (PCF) adopted a generally unsympathetic and conservative role towards the series of popular protests and demonstrations involving students and workers which took place between 3 May and 1 June. Indeed, it has been suggested that all the organised opposition parties, the PCF, the Federation of the Left (FGDS) and the Left-Wing Socialist Party (PSU), had no conception of what was happening during the first two weeks of May, since the events concerned were beyond their political frame of reference. Ultimately the fragile alliance between students and workers was broken by the Gaullist government and the communist-dominated trade union federation (CGT) persuading workers to end their protests and to return to work.

Throughout this period the PCF had adopted a conservative position, having determined that the conditions were not 'ripe' for radical social change and that the form taken by the popular protests and rebellions was 'adventurist' (cf. Posner, 1970). However, it would seem that the hostility of the PCF was not entirely a matter of a principled objection to strategy or a consequence of a different analysis of the 'balance of forces', but rather that it represented a manifestation of the self-interest of the organisation. There existed a strong feeling within the leadership of the party that its organisation was being challenged by the upsurge of popular protest and the emergence of inform- ally organised groupings. Nevertheless, whatever the reasons for the response of the PCF to the events of May '68, there seems to be a high degree of unanimity amongst commentators that 'The restraint exercised by the Communist leadership was ... even more effective than governmental resistance' (Glucks- mann, 1970, p. 185). Undoubtedly the contribution of the PCF and the CGT to the termination of the May movement constituted something of a revelation for those people who had associated these organisations with a radical and progressive politics, and furthermore it served as a powerful reminder of the possible conservatism of Marxist political parties. In addition it raised the spectre of conservative tendencies within Marxist theory.

The emergence of new 'social subjects' or new political group- ings, 'groupuscles', around specific issues, such as education, women's liberation, ecology, gay liberation, prisoners' rights, and so forth, has, especially since May '68, constituted a prob- lem for conventional Marxist political analysis. The tendency to conceptualise politics in terms of class politics and thereby to reduce the political to the level of class relations, class alliances and class struggle has proven less than satisfactory, causing some Marxist theoreticians to consider alternative non-Marxist conceptualisations of power and politics (cf. Poulantzas, 1978). The emergence of new 'social subjects' has also drawn attention to the limitations of conceptualising effective modes of political association as equivalent to hierarchical forms of political organisation and to the associated problem of the relationship, or lack of such, between, on the one hand, the political organi- sation and its membership and, on the other hand, the political organisation or party and other constituencies. One of the implications of May '68 was that the institutionalised organisa- tions of political opposition were unable to represent a sizeable fraction of their membership and were even less capable of comprehending, let alone representing, the interests, wishes and desires of those people who expressed themselves through participation in new political groupings.

Whether we are to regard the events of May '68 as a success or a failure is a matter of debate. If we attribute to the parti- cipants an intention to radically transform the social order then perhaps it is appropriate to talk of failure. In that case we come

close to an endorsement of the official PCF position, namely that
the time was not right and that the events were the product of
'political adventurism'. On the other hand, it may equally well
be argued that the events of May '68 constituted not only a
critique of the existing social order but in addition a de facto
critique of institutionalised and hierarchically organised forms
of political opposition, and that in so far as Marxist theory and
related forms of political organisation were indeed revealed to
be problematic then the events may not be regarded as a failure.
Although May '68 was much less than a revolution in the conventional sense of that term, by which I mean that no attempt
was made to destroy or to seize state power, it did nevertheless
constitute a challenge to the social order. Several fundamental
aspects of social life were challenged, including the legitimacy
of ruling and oppositional institutions; models of production,
consumption and information; as well as established rules,
beliefs and customs. The May movement initiated a critique
which

> questioned the 'organizational viewpoint', which orders our
> world by parcelling out social life and labelling individuals....
> [It] opened a *breach* in the technocratic-bourgeois order.
> The depth of this breach was such that, however brief its
> duration, it shook the bureaucracy of the so-called Left,
> which, in at least one of its wings, is the potential home of
> totalitarianism. (Lefort, 1978, p. 37)

Despite a general restoration of the 'old order', the effects of
the May movement have not been erased; its legacy is present
in new modes of social and political thought and in the new
forms of politics and social struggle which have emerged since
1968 and which in their turn stand in a relationship of opposition to the 'further homogenization of society and its technical
rationalization' (ibid.).

The other event which we may situate at the epicentre of the
current crisis of Marxism is, as I have already noted, that of
the 'Prague Spring'. Undoubtedly, the events in Czechoslovakia
in 1968, the 'Prague Spring' and its aftermath, constitute something of a watershed for Western socialists and for Western
communist parties, for the possibility of the construction of a
humane form of socialism, 'socialism with a human face', was
crushed in the name of friendship and in the cause of the
restoration of an impoverished and bureaucratically regulated
system of oppression. With this event the rationale for the
societies of 'actually existing socialism' has been more difficult
to sustain, although there have been some 'noble' attempts.
Admission of the regular violation of human rights in the USSR
and in other Eastern European states; of the growing economic
crisis in Comecon (cf. Carlo, 1980); of the existence of powerful and privileged ruling strata in the societies of 'actually
existing socialism'; and of the barbarity of the various forms of

military intervention which have been explained as necessary
to preserve socialism (e.g. East Germany 1953, Hungary 1956,
Czechoslovakia 1968, Afghanistan 1979, Poland 1981), has been
difficult to resist, and has contributed to the emergence of
a critical examination of Soviet-style socialism, of the form of
social, political and economic life in the societies of actually
existing socialism, and finally, because it is implicated, of
Marxism itself.

Although the 'Prague Spring' and its aftermath may serve as
yet another illustration of an indefensible intervention by the
Soviet Union in the internal affairs of an independent state,
albeit a member state within the Warsaw Pact, the responses
elicited from the Western European communist parties did not
conform to type: whereas the invasion of Hungary in 1956 had
been largely tolerated, the invasion of Czechoslovakia was not.
Indeed, it has been argued that the destruction of Dubcek's
communism by the Soviet invasion was synonymous with the
birth of Eurocommunism (cf. Levi, 1979), for the myths of the
social, economic, political and moral superiority of the Soviet
Union were no longer sustainable. It is from this moment that
we can trace the growth of fundamental differences between
the communist parties of East and West, differences which have
been articulated in the form of conceptions of democratic roads
to socialism (e.g. by the communist parties of Italy (PCI),
Spain (PCE) and Great Britain (CPGB)) and these, in turn,
have been associated with quite radical examinations and reformulations of Marxist theory.

It is not difficult to understand that the events of 1968 and
their associated developments should have precipitated a crisis
of Marxism. The conventional response within Marxism to problems of theory and practice has been to return to first principles, to the classical texts of the tradition, to work out, or
perhaps more appropriately, to discover a solution. Such a
response, of course, represents merely one option and it is
predicated on the assumption that a solution may be generated
from within a Marxist problematic. Alternatively, it might be
argued that the respective problems and limitations do not admit
of a solution within a Marxist problematic, in other words, that
the various schools of Marxist thought, each attempting to
formulate the definitive Marxist analysis, achieve nothing more
than a restatement of the problems. As Bobbio has remarked:

> Instead of proceeding, as would any scientist who attempts
> to substitute adequate for inadequate theory, the doctrinaire
> follows the opposite path, that of substituting a 'correct' for
> a necessarily incorrect interpretation of the doctrine. There-
> fore it comes to pass that a doctrine's fate is characterized
> not by one theory succeeding another, but by differing inter-
> pretations of the text clashing with one another. (1979a,
> p. 192)

Hence we encounter a plethora of schools or sects (e.g. existential, phenomenological, structuralist Marxism, etc.), each addressing and claiming to resolve the problems of Marxism.

However, beneath the apparent differences between the respective schools and analyses of Western Marxism there remain the unresolved limitations and problems which have been inherited from the classical Marxist tradition (cf. Anderson, 1976). It is to these problems and limitations as they have been manifested within Marxist theory that I will turn first.

PROBLEMS OF THEORY

The relationship between Marxist theory and the pattern or sequence of historical events has never been simple or straightforward. The October Revolution, the continual adaptability of the capitalist mode of production, changes in the social class structure, the rise of new political groupings and a variety of other developments have, at different moments, brought into question the conception of a relationship between Marxist theoretical analysis and the pattern of historical events. Not infrequently, some might argue too often (cf. Bobbio, 1979a), it has been history or the event rather than theory or analysis that has been regarded as out of step or in 'error', or alternatively the limitations of analysis have been treated as the product of errors of interpretation or of readings of the texts. A different and more credible response to the evident distance between Marxist theory and the sequence of historical events is that such a gap is inevitable. In one instance it has been argued that this distance 'between theory and the real holds good for every theory, including Marxism' (cf. Poulantzas, 1978, p. 22), in another that 'there will ... always remain an inherent scissiparity between knowledge and action, theory and practice' (cf. Anderson, 1976, p. 110). To pursue this issue further we necessarily have to consider the question of the epistemological grounds of Marxism, namely the question of its scientificity.

The question of science and scientific method has become an increasingly significant issue within Marxist theory. The authority vested in or claimed for Marxism has almost always been grounded upon, or derived from, conceptions of the validity or 'truth' of the analyses it has generated, and ultimately behind these conceptions of validity or truth there has been a conception of the scientific grounds of Marxism. The extent to which attempts have been made to establish the scientific grounds of Marxist analysis has varied throughout the history of Marxist thought, although it seems to have become an issue of increasing significance within the tradition of Western Marxism, that tradition which began with attempts to account for the disparity between Marxist theory, the Russian Revolution and its controversial aftermath. Increasingly the question of the epistemo-

logical grounds and methodological basis of Marxism has become
associated with a general debate over the epistemological and
methodological status of the human or social sciences (cf. Therborn, 1976). However, the principal source of the controversy
over the question of the scientificity of Marxism lies with Marx's
work, so we should proceed from there.

The roots of Marxism lie in the nineteenth century, and the
predominant conception of scientificity informing the Marxist
tradition has been derived from that era. Moral values and political preferences may have featured to a greater or lesser degree
in the works of Marx and Engels, but it has generally been
argued that the true value of their works, their authority so to
speak, has been derived from the epistemological status of their
analyses. It is the assumed scientific status of their analyses
which has provided the authority for the formulation of political
programmes, plans and social policies. However, the question of
the scientific grounds of Marxism has proven no less controversial or difficult to resolve than any of the other conceptual
issues. Furthermore, the absence of any sustained consideration
of scientific methodology within Marx's work has given a free
rein to committed imaginations and has thereby licensed all
manner of speculation.

On this issue we may make a distinction between those explanations or accounts of the work of Marx, his method and conception of science, which seek to affirm or to establish its
revolutionary or distinctive character (cf. Althusser, 1969;
Althusser and Balibar, 1972), and those other explanations or
accounts which identify a high degree of comparability between
the conception of science and scientific method present within
the works of Marx and other nineteenth-century conceptions of
science (cf. Fletcher, 1974, p. 52; Habermas, 1974). Now, if
we proceed from the works of Marx and Engels and their direct
references to science, it is evident that their respective conceptions had a considerable affinity with conceptions in the
fields of the natural and biological sciences. We might state that
their conceptions of science were formulated in the shadow of
Darwin (cf. Marx, 1976a, pp. 100-2; 1977, p. 525; Engels, 1971,
p. 46) and that an assumption which consistently underpinned
their work was that the object of their analysis, namely the
condition and process of transformation of the capitalist mode
of production, might be 'determined with the precision of natural
science' (Marx, 1977, p. 389). Reference to the epistemological
and historical context in which Marxism emerged has provided
the framework within which it has been argued that Marx
employed a positivist conception of science (cf. Wellmer, 1974).

The central features of the positivist conception of science
identified within the work of Marx have not escaped criticism.
Indeed, the presence of such a conception in the works of Marx
and Engels has been identified as the primary source of the
limitations of Marxist political practice (cf. Habermas, 1974).
The positivistic conception of science identified within Marx's

analysis has been considered to be synonymous with an assumption of the possibility of a technical mastery being exercised
not only over natural processes but in addition over social and
cultural processes and events. Implicit within such a positivist
conception of science is an assumption that the social domain,
social processes and social events are amenable to regulation
and control through social technologies. The test of analysis,
its validity, may then be held to lie with the degree of success
with which social processes and events are subordinated to
management, regulation or control, the latter being revealed
in practice. An assumption of this order is not peculiar to
Marxism, it constitutes a fundamental feature of social scientific
inquiry which seeks to legitimate its existence in terms of its
revelation of the etiology of social processes and events, or
what amounts to much the same thing, in terms of its provision
of a form of knowledge which may provide a basis for social
policy, planning and intervention. Moreover, we should be careful not to conclude that such forms of analysis and inquiry
necessarily have negative consequences, for in general terms
such work may be productively associated with the provision of
benefits, an amelioration of the human condition and reform of
iniquitous social practices. However, in the particular case of
Marxism and its theorisation of the laws of motion of the capitalist mode of production and associated forms of political practice
there have been grounds for concern. The most significant of
these has been the apparent contradiction between the conception of science on which Marxist analysis is predicated and a
political interest in the realisation of human emancipation, towards which Marxism seems to be directed. Within Marxism the
formulations arising from theory or analysis and the possibility
of the implementation in practice of any programmes of action
constructed from such analysis are directly associated with
the institutionalised figure of the political party. Conventionally
it is the party which has ownership of what may be described
as the alternative understanding or the 'counter-truth'. It is
the party which embodies the necessary mechanism through
which positive social changes may be engineered and behind
which the masses may be drawn or guided towards their destiny.
In consequence it has been argued, for example by the critical
theorists (cf. Habermas, 1974; Wellmer, 1974), that the presence of a positivist conception of science within the works of
Marx had, and has continued to have, consequences for the
articulation of a Marxist politics. In particular it has meant that
an interest in the realisation of enlightenment and human emancipation has, at best, been transformed through the employment
of instrumental forms of reasoning and associated technicist conceptions of the social world into centrally organised and directed
programmes of political intervention which may yield a change in
political power, if not in its form, and which may in addition
initiate some measure of social reform. At worst it may be argued
that a Marxist programme guarantees only that one form of state

power may be displaced by another, more powerful form which has appropriated the authority of science.

Within Marxism, as I have attempted to indicate, there has been a degree of ambivalance over the relationship between forms of theorising, political practices and events. Sometimes it seems as though the relationship has been conceptualised as one of correspondence, either actual – that is to say, there have been historical moments in which a correspondence has been achieved, perhaps the October Revolution may be regarded as an example (cf. Hoffman, 1975) – or alternatively as a potential which may be realised in an indeterminate future (cf. Anderson, 1976, p. 104). Now, although not all Marxists would subscribe to the view outlined here – for example, the idea of any correspondence between theory and practice seems to have been rejected by Poulantzas – I believe that the formulation or the assumption of a relationship of some kind between specific historical events and Marxist theory has constituted a central feature of Marxism. Indeed, it is difficult to comprehend that criticisms of the Soviet Union and of the other societies of actually existing socialism should have precipitated a crisis of Marxism other than in terms of a conception of some kind of relationship between Marxist theory and events. Criticisms of these societies have constituted criticisms of the 'model' for socialism and, in turn, this has led to the expression of concern as to whether socialism is at all possible, and to even more fundamental questions concerning the very idea of socialism. Concomitantly the realisation that the societies of actually existing socialism no longer constitute a good model has had consequences for Marxist theory. First, assuming a close relationship between theory and the sequence of events concerned, then the limitations of the societies of actually existing socialism have been attributed to inadequacies in Marxist theory, hence Marxism has been held responsible for the form of life in Eastern Europe (e.g. the 'Gulag question'). Alternatively, it has been argued that the emergence of the societies of actually existing socialism and their respective form of life was largely unforeseen or unanticipated by Marxist theory, that Marxism lacked and continues to lack adequate concepts for analysing these societies. In other words the societies of actually existing socialism testify to the limits of Marxist theory; they serve to weaken the claims of global relevance claimed for Marxism by reminding us of the partiality of Marxist theory towards an analysis of the capitalist mode of production.

Although I have located the re-emergence of a crisis of Marxism in the events of 1968 it is evident that this crisis has a long pedigree and may even be considered synonymous with the history of Marxism itself. Certainly, if the events of 1968 are considered to constitute the historical moment at which the crisis of Marxism re-emerged, the roots of the crisis lie elsewhere in earlier theoretical and political events. One particular event which has achieved a degree of significance is the

Twentieth Congress of the Communist Party of the Soviet Union
at which Khrushchev sought to 'settle accounts' with Stalin.
This event has constituted something of a watershed for Marxism
in so far as the explanation of Stalin's crimes through the
deployment of a conception of the 'cult of personality', simultaneously cast doubt on the validity of historical materialism and
on the functioning of the Soviet system. For, as Feuer has
commented, 'if the "cult of personality" was founded on a single
individual, then historical materialism was false; but if the "cult"
arose from the Soviet system, then socialist society itself must
bear the responsibility for the inherent potential of Stalinism'
(1971, p. 40). From this moment on the crisis of Marxism has
steadily developed, for it was here that an admission was made
that there might be an unacceptable face of socialism. Furthermore, Khrushchev's indictment of the Stalinist 'terror' was also
an admission that the party had been in error. From such
'lessons of history' there have emerged not only the political
events of 1968, the attempt to construct a 'socialism with a
human face', the spontaneous irruption of non-bureaucratic
forms of popular political protest, and the subsequent articulation of alternative democratic routes to socialism on the part of
Western European communist parties, but in addition, attempts
to repair the damage inflicted upon Marxism – attempts which
have generally taken the form of, or have been closely associated
with, an examination of the fundamental premises of Marxist
analysis. There has, in consequence, been a regeneration of
Marxist theory.

Over the past two decades or so there has been a dramatic
increase in contributions in the field of Marxist theory, philosophy and method. However, one particular contribution has
achieved a singular degree of significance, namely that originating with the work of Althusser. To a greater or lesser extent
each of the different contributions to Marxist theory in this
period may be regarded as addressing, or debating with, the
Althusserian position. Therefore, by taking the latter as our
principal focus, not only will we be able to reconsider the most
rigorous of attempts to clarify and resolve the central problems
confronting Marxist theory, but in addition we will be able to
take note of the extent to which these problems have remained
unresolved and have continued to constitute a source of controversy.

FROM EXISTENTIALISM TO STRUCTURALISM

The significance of the Twentieth Congress of the CPSU was
not that it revealed for the first time the crimes and errors
perpetrated in the name of Stalin but rather that it served to
retrospectively legitimate many of the criticisms coded within
the various developments in Marxist theory which had emerged
after the death of Lenin. The aftermath of the October Revolu-

tion, the rise of Stalinism and the concomitant relative stability
of the Western capitalist societies was the general context in
which Western Marxism developed. This is the context in which
a 'divorce' between theory and practice became evident (cf.
Anderson, 1976). It is to this historical conjuncture that we
may trace the preoccupation with theory and philosophy within
contemporary Marxism and the series of attempts to establish the
scientificity of historical materialism. The apparent vitality of
the bourgeois order and the Stalinisation of the communist movement simultaneously produced a crisis for socialist culture and
a regeneration of bourgeois thought. The rapid development and
increasing heterogeneity of Marxist theory have constituted a
response to these events. As Anderson has remarked, 'The
original relationship between Marxist theory and proletarian
practice was subtly but steadily substituted by a new relationship between Marxist theory and bourgeois theory' (1976, p. 55).
This relationship has assumed the form of both an engagement
or a conflict within theory, between 'Marxist' and 'bourgeois'
tendencies, and a degree of mutual influence, which in the case
of Marxism has taken the form of a series of attempts to reconcile particular forms of non-Marxist philosophy with historical
materialism.
    I will not attempt to document each of these formal shifts
(cf. Anderson, 1976) but will instead concentrate on one particular shift, which may be conceptualised in terms of a movement
from existentialist to structuralist positions within Marxism. The
development of existential, phenomenological and humanist forms
of Marxism constituted a response to the apparent scientism of
classical Marxism. These developments may be regarded as a
reaction to the perceived limitations of both Marxist theory and
politics, namely to 'positivist' and 'economist' tendencies within
Marxist theory and to the absence of any realisation of the
political promise of Marxism. A common theme within existential,
phenomenological and humanist forms of Marxism has been a
return to, or a restoration of, a conception of 'man makes
history', for which the discovery of the writings of the 'young'
Marx, notably the 'Economic and Philosophic Manuscripts of
1844', has been of special significance. These manuscripts have
constituted a reference point for several generations of Marxist
theoreticians: for some they have been of positive value in their
respective reformulations of historical materialism (e.g. Lukács,
Marcuse, Lefebvre, Merleau-Ponty, Sartre and Paci), whilst
for others the very same manuscripts have become an object of
criticism or a negative reference for the development of a radically different 'structuralist' reformulation of historical materialism (cf. Althusser, 1969).
    It was in the 1960s that the influence of structuralism became
prominent and eventually took the form of a project to establish
the scientific grounds of Marxism. In the case of existential,
phenomenological and humanist forms of Marxism a conception of
human experience, or the conscious subject, is situated at the

centre of social and historical processes. The emergence of
structuralism effectively transformed the intellectual milieu and
thereby directly challenged prevailing humanist conceptions
and analyses. Within structuralist thought man is 'decentred'
from his own meanings, and the conscious subject is no longer
located at the centre of social activity. With the advent of
structuralist thought there occurred a movement from 'subject'
to 'structure', from the view that human beings are the creators
of their world to the view that human beings are the product
of structures, formed by or within hidden or unconscious
structures (e.g. kinship, myth and desire).

The impact of contemporary structuralist thought upon Marxism is most evident in the work of Althusser. Althusser set
out to rescue Marxism from what were termed the bourgeois
deviations of economism and humanism. His project took the
form of an attempt to demonstrate the scientificity of Marxism,
to establish the scientific grounds of Marxist analysis. In brief,
Althusser argued that Marx was responsible for an immense
scientific revolution, that with 'Capital' the continent of history
had been opened up for scientific analysis. Althusser's task was
to explicate that of which Marx and Engels had been unaware,
namely the epistemological significance of their advance. Establishing the form of the perceived qualitative leap or advance
thus constituted for Althusser a vital theoretical and political
task.

Of necessity, Althusser's reading of the works of Marx and
Engels sought to settle accounts with alternative readings,
notably 'humanist' readings. For example he has stated:

> Marx's theoretical anti-humanism, as it operates within
> historical materialism, thus means a refusal to root the
> explanation of social formations and their history in a con-
> cept of man with theoretical pretensions, that is, a concept
> of man as an *originating subject*, one in whom originate his
> needs (*homo oeconomicus*), his thoughts (*homo rationalis*),
> and his acts and struggles (*homo moralis, juridicus* and
> *politicus*). (1976, p. 205)

Althusser arrived at this conception of Marx's theoretical anti-
humanism through a reading which differentiated between the
writings of the 'young' Marx, contaminated by idealist philosophy, and the mature works such as 'Capital', which were
considered to reveal the seeds of a new science of history.

In Althusser's view the validity of Marxist analysis, its superiority over bourgeois thought, had not yet been established by
'official' Marxists or by humanist Marxists. Hence the importance
of the task to establish the independent 'truth value' of Marxism. Integral to the establishment of the validity or superiority
of Marxist thought was the necessity of demonstrating that the
process of production of knowledge was clinically isolated from
ethical, moral and political interests. For Althusser the scienti-

ficity of Marxism rested with its production of a system of logically related concepts, which might reveal the hidden structure of the capitalist mode of production. The validity of theory was not to be confirmed through political practice; rather it was to be established internally, according to rational criteria. Ultimately Althusser's attempt to confirm the scientificity of Marxism came to grief over the problem of establishing the grounds on which science might be differentiated from non-science (or ideology). An attempt at differentiating science from non-science lies at the heart of the Althusserian project and two versions may be found in his work.

The first formulation of a distinction between science and non-science took the form of a rationalist distinction between science and ideology, a fundamental contrast of truth and error. The scientificity of Marxism was conceptualised in terms of an 'epistemological break' or rupture with bourgeois ideology. This 'break' was presented by Althusser as a theoretical fact and was in turn affirmed through specific references to the texts of Marx and Engels. Althusser's thesis was that a fundamental shift may be detected within Marx's work, that the 'Theses on Feuerbach' and 'The German Ideology' provided the first signs of a new problematic which was initially developed in such 'transitional works' as the 'Manifesto' and 'The Poverty of Philosophy' and subsequently in the 'mature works'. These works which emerged after the 'epistemological break' of 1845 revealed not only the presence of new theoretical concepts but the absence of others which had been a feature of the writings of the 'young' Marx (e.g. conceptions of human essence, alienation, etc.). Now, although Althusser has subsequently qualified this position he has retained a conception of a fundamental shift of emphasis being present within Marx's work. This is described as

> a 'change of terrain' ... a new terrain on which the new concepts, after much elaboration, can lay down the foundations of a *scientific* theory, or ... 'open the road' to the development of what will, irresistibly become a science, an unusual science, a *revolutionary science*, but a theory which contains what we recognize in the sciences, because it provides *objective knowledge*. (Althusser, 1976, p. 110).

However, Althusser's problem was not to assert the scientificity of Marxism but rather to demonstrate its emergence and to distinguish it from 'the classical positivist or vulgar, bourgeois picture'. This has proven more difficult.

A second formulation of the distinction between science and non-science has emerged from Althusser's process of self-criticism. The science-ideology antithesis has been rejected as a 'theoreticist error'. Althusser has proceeded to argue that an analysis has to be attempted of the conditions under which the 'new science' emerged. The analysis offered draws heavily upon

the works of Engels and Lenin and their identification of the
conjunction within which Marxism emerged, namely a conjunction
of 'theoretical elements', German philosophy, English political
economy and French socialism, and 'practical realities' such as
transformations in the mode of production and associated class
struggles. The question of the emergence of the 'science of
history' is, in this instance, not posed in terms of a rationalist
distinction between science and ideology; rather it has taken the
form of an examination of how and why 'this ideological *conjunction* could produce a scientific *disjunction*' (Althusser, 1976,
p. 157). Furthermore, the answer generated by Althusser does
not make reference to purely epistemological grounds, but
instead proceeds with a reference to the adoption by Marx of
'new proletarian class positions' as the first element of an
answer.

The adoption of proletarian positions by Marx has been conceptualised as a necessary but not a sufficient condition for the
emergence of the science of history, for such proletarian class
positions had to be worked out into a theoretical position before
the new science could develop. In this revised version of the
emergence of the science of history the conception of an 'epistemological break' does not disappear from the analysis; rather
it is displaced by the conceptualisation of Marx's political position as the determinant element. Briefly, the developments to
which Althusser has made reference include approximately parallel shifts in the political positions (from 'radical bourgeois
liberalism to petty bourgeois humanism then to communism') and
philosophical positions (from idealism to philosophical materialism
to a revolutionary materialism) embodied in the works of Marx
as well as in the objects of his analyses (from 'Law to the State,
then to Political Economy'). We are informed that the political
position may have assumed the determinant place but that, in
turn, the philosophical position was no less important for it
constituted the mode of expression or articulation of the politics.

If Althusser's theoretical detour constituted an attempt to
underwrite the scientificity of Marxism, then it must be considered a failure, for what has emerged from the Althusserian
project has not been a demonstration but rather, at best, a
reaffirmation of the scientificity of Marxism. The earlier 'theoreticist error' has simply been replaced with an analysis which
returns to a conception of the union between theory and practice. Thus Althusser has concluded that the appearance of the
science of history was made possible by Marx's adoption of a
proletarian political position which was subsequently articulated
in theory. However, this leaves the question of the grounds of
the scientificity of Marxism unresolved; indeed, it might be
argued that the whole issue has been exacerbated by the failure
of the Althusserian project. Furthermore, as a consequence of
the special claim made for Marx's 'mature' analysis, namely that
it manifests a break with 'all ideological conceptions' and denotes
the emergence of a science of history, the establishment of its

singularity or difference from other analyses has become an
issue of even greater significance. If such a claim is to be made
for Marxism then its distinctiveness has to be established. It is
not sufficient to assert that its truth or validity may be derived
from a possible union between 'proletarian positions' in theory
and politics. Alternatively, such seemingly insoluble problems
may be avoided by rejecting the very notion of Marxism as
science (cf. Thompson, 1978, p. 360).

FROM STRUCTURALISM TO 'HUMAN EXPERIENCE'

The response to Althusser's work within Marxism has been somewhat mixed. On the one hand there have been positive responses
by contemporary Marxists who have proceeded to embrace substantial elements of Althusser's work (e.g. Poulantzas), yet on
the other hand there have been fiercely critical responses from
Marxists who have claimed that Althusser has merely produced
an 'academic fiction' (e.g. Thompson, 1978). I will continue
my account of the theoretical controversies at the heart of the
crisis of Marxism by making reference to particular points on
which Thompson takes issue with Althusser. My comparison is
not intended to be exhaustive, nor could it be, given the
complexity of the issues involved. I merely wish to abstract the
dichotomies or dimensions along or in terms of which significant
differences may be noted, not only between the respective positions of Althusser and Thompson, but more generally between
contributions to the debate on the nature of a Marxist analysis.
    Thompson's reading of the classical Marxist tradition differs
considerably from that of Althusser. Thompson's view is that
the basis of historical materialism is a 'unitary knowledge of
society' and that such a reading may be derived from an evaluation of specific texts, namely the 'Economic and Philosophic
Manuscripts of 1844', 'The German Ideology', 'The Poverty of
Philosophy' and the 'Communist Manifesto', texts which represent the genuine embodiment of Marx's project. In Thompson's
work Marxism does not assume the status of a theory and the
claims made for its scientificity are considered to be spurious.
Instead the emphasis has been placed upon another tradition, of
open empirical inquiry and historical analysis, which, not
unlike the 'scientific tradition' addressed by Althusser, may
also be derived from the work of Marx. Indeed, Thompson has
gone further by arguing that the construction of a unitary
knowledge of society has constituted the true objective of
historical materialism and that we may therefore regard Marx's
writings on political economy as something of a departure from
genuine historical materialism. Furthermore, in so far as Althusser has sought to elevate the very analyses which are most
removed from the true objective of historical materialism, then
the errors arising from Marx's engagement with political economy
are compounded. In Thompson's view we may identify Marx's

preoccupation with political economy as the principal source of the subsequent problem of economic determination and the associated controversy over the question of human agency. The general error attributed to Marx by Thompson, namely a disproportionate focus on the capitalist mode of production to the detriment of empirical social formations, is, in turn, considered to have been further exacerbated by the singular emphasis in Althusser's work on the mode of production. Hence Thompson's general antipathy towards the Althusserian project.

In the course of the redirection of Marxism towards its true objective, the construction of a unitary knowledge of society, Thompson has indicated that a particular problem has become evident, namely the absence of a concept through which to account for the articulation of modes of production with historical process. The appropriate concept is deemed to be that of 'human experience'. Thus the articulation between a determinate mode of production and a particular historical process is embodied in human experience, or, in Thompson's terms, the correspondence between a mode of production and historical process comes about through

> persons experiencing their determinate productive situations and relationships, as needs and interests and as antagonisms, and then 'handling' this experience within their *consciousness* and their *culture* (... terms excluded by theoretical practice) in the most complex (yes, 'relatively autonomous') ways, and then ... acting upon their determinate situation in their turn. (Thompson, 1978, p. 356)

Thereby, in contrast to the structuralist decentring of the subject, exemplified within Marxism by Althusser's work, Thompson has reinstated men and women within history.

The virtue of Thompson's concept of human experience seems to be that it enables the theorist or the historian to address and possibly even to explain the various transitions and modifications in society which were quite deliberately excluded from Marx's analysis of the capitalist mode of production. What Thompson has in mind are

> all those dense, complex and elaborated systems by which familial and social life is structured and social consciousness finds realisation and expression ... all of which, in their sum, comprise the 'genetics' of the whole historical process, all of them joined, at a certain point, in common human experience, which itself ... exerts its pressure on the sum. (Ibid., pp. 362-3)

However, there are one or two problems associated with the concept of experience advanced by Thompson. First, given the significance it assumes, the concept remains relatively underdeveloped (cf. Anderson, 1980, p. 80). Second, where reference

is made to the concept the indications are that it is constituted
as the genetic code of history. This signifies a radical departure
from the central tenets of historical materialism, for which the
contradiction between the forces and social relations of production has constituted the locus of historical change. It has been
remarked that a 'creeping culturalism', evident in Thompson's
comments on the silences and exclusions in Marx's work and in
his concomitant development of appropriate concepts, is indicative of a liberal rather than a Marxist position (cf. Thompson,
1978, pp. 360-3; Anderson, 1980, pp. 82-3). In other words
Thompson's response to the limitations of Marx's analysis of
the capitalist mode of production and to the subsequent development of this analysis as synonymous with historical materialism,
as for example in the Althusserian project, has taken him beyond
the limits of a Marxist problematic.

Now, although this may, in Anderson's view, constitute a
weakness, it would seem that for Thompson it constitutes merely
a corollary of the view that 'Marxism no longer has anything to
tell us of the world, nor any way of finding out ... [and that]
Marx was often wrong, and sometimes wrong in damaging ways'
(Thompson, 1978, pp. 360-1). Thompson has not been concerned
either with the development of Marxism and its several schools
or with a cultivation of what Marx might have intended to say;
rather his reference has been to a critical tradition of open,
empirical inquiry which, although it may be derived from Marx's
work, does not terminate with it. Thompson may still talk of
practising as a Marxist, but it is clear that the reference is to
an open, critical Marxist tradition, rather than to a 'pursuit of
the security of a perfect totalised theory' (ibid., p. 357).

For Thompson, Marxism is not, then, the science of history,
but one of the interpretive systems in historiography that have
yet to be disproven, or one of the legitimate ways of inter-
rogating historical materials. From this point of view, the more
Marxism has been confined within the discourse of political
economy, the less it has been able to develop a unitary knowledge of society. Thus Thompson has identified the preoccupation with scientificity, the concomitant necessary reference to
and development of analysis within the discourse of political
economy, and the associated prevalence of economism, as
fundamental limitations of the Marxist tradition. These limitations
have manifested themselves in the form of a conflation of knowledge with science and the submission of all other knowledges
to the measure of Marxist science, and in the form of analyses
which have generalised from 'Capital' to capitalism. As Thompson has noted, this error derives from Marx's drift

> from *Capital* (an abstraction of Political Economy, which is
> his proper concern) to *capitalism* ('the complicated bour-
> geois system'), that is, the whole society conceived of as
> an 'organic system'. But the whole society comprises many
> activities and relations (of power, of consciousness, sexual,

cultural, normative) which are not the concern of Political
Economy, which have been *defined out of* Political Economy,
and for which it has no terms. (Ibid., p. 254)

One important consequence of this tendency to generalise from
'Capital' to capitalism has emerged within the Marxist tradition
in the form of the problem of determination.

Before turning to the issue of determination, however, we
might take note of the two major axes which constantly recur
within the Marxist tradition and in terms of which the general
positions of Althusser and Thompson may be differentiated.
These are, respectively, first an emphasis on system or structure in contrast to human agency, subjectivity and consciousness, and second a prioritising of scientificity and 'causal
knowledge' over and above other forms of knowledge, moral
values and experience (cf. Thompson, 1978, pp. 363-4). For
Thompson the value of the Marxist tradition seems to rest more
with its possible provision of what may be termed ethical models,
which may enable us to identify with others in the past, to learn
and to receive inspiration from them, the better to exercise
our own (assumed) powers of action in the present, than with
the pursuit of a form of causal knowledge, itself inappropriate,
which it has been assumed may constitute an adequate basis for
political practice in the present. The latter type of analysis,
as Thompson has warned, points towards 'system and "science"
in ways which afford uncomfortable continuities to the isms and
State ideologies of our time' (ibid., p. 361).

ON DETERMINATION

A specific reference to a Marxist analysis or approach is indicative of a qualitative difference from alternative approaches or of
the existence of a relatively specific tradition, one which displays common features or draws upon common principles. One
such principle, which has informed work within the several
schools of Marxism and which, in turn, may be traced back
through a broad range of interpretations to Marx's work, is that
of determination. The importance assumed by this principle
within the Marxist tradition may be gauged from Stuart Hall's
comment: 'When we leave the terrain of "determination" we
desert not just this or that stage in Marx's thought, but his
whole problematic' (1977, p. 52). The implication here is that
the distinctiveness and the specificity of a Marxist analysis is
inextricably bound up with a principle of determination.
Furthermore, in so far as Marxist analysis has developed,
broadly speaking, within the conceptual framework of political
economy, then determination has been conceptualised as in the
final instance 'economic'. In consequence, Marxist analyses
have tended to conceptualise phenomena in terms of either a
direct or an indirect relationship of economic determination.

The conception of economic determination has been a source of considerable controversy within the Marxist tradition. Both conceptions, of the 'economic' and of 'determination', have suffered from the high degree of ambiguity present in the texts of the classical tradition. I have already made reference to the criticism that Marx's analyses, in particular in 'Capital', became progressively marked by the concepts and categories of his antagonists and that as such his work did not constitute 'an exercise of a different order to that of mature bourgeois Political Economy, but a total confrontation *within* that order' (Thompson, 1978, p. 257). One of the consequences of the internal character of Marx's critique has been evident in the absence of appropriate concepts with which to theorise a wide range of fundamental social practices and relations and the associated reduction of such practices and relations to an epiphenomenal status of the economic. An additional and related difficulty has been the apparent conflation of the concepts of production and economy articulated in Marx's work.

Laclau (1977) has argued that Marx employed two quite different conceptions of the economic. One conception 'defines one of the conditions of every possible society' (ibid., p. 75), and here the economic is synonymous with production; the other conception has a more specific reference, namely to commodity-producing societies only. The first conception may be regarded as integral to the formulation of the general premises of historical materialism outlined by Marx in the famous 1859 Preface to 'A Contribution to the Critique of Political Economy', namely that 'The mode of production of material life determines the general character of the social, political, and spiritual process of life'. The second conception of 'the economic' has as its reference 'the sphere of commodities, the market' (Laclau, 1977, p. 75) and therefore its relevance is confined to the analysis of the capitalist mode of production. Laclau has argued that the unity of these two conceptions of the economic is a peculiarity of the capitalist mode of production, and further that it is only in this specific instance, namely where economy (viz. production of commodities) is 'identified with the basic productive relations of the society' (ibid., p. 77), that the economic may be conceptualised as determinant.

Many of the problems and controversies which have arisen around the concept of determination have been a consequence of misguided generalisations based upon analyses of the capitalist mode of production which have been applied to non-capitalist modes of production. This is the context in which Laclau has proposed a distinction between the two conceptions of 'the economic', employing the concept 'production' for the first expression and retaining the concept of 'the economic' for the second. The advantage of this proposal is that it simultaneously allows a distinction to be made between the capitalist mode of production, where economy may be conceptualised as determinant, and non-capitalist modes of production, where the economic

is not determinant, without undermining the now even more
general premise of historical materialism, namely that the production of material existence constitutes the level of determination. However, the problem with this formulation is that the
conception is potentially so broad as to encompass all manner of
analyses, thereby making Marxists of us all. In so far as the
concept of the production of material existence is open to a
variety of interpretations, ranging from the provision of basic
needs as outlined in 'The German Ideology' to the more general
(re)production of a 'way of life' (cf. Williams, 1977, pp. 90-4),
then the 'terrain of determinations' will continue to be a source
of great controversy.

The various conceptions and formulations of determination
within contemporary Marxist thought have been derived from
particular interpretations of selected works of Marx and Engels.
Perhaps the most significant works have been 'The German
Ideology'; the 1859 Preface; 'The Eighteenth Brumaire of Louis
Bonaparte'; 'Capital'; and the letters of Engels to Bloch
(21-2 September 1890), Schmidt (27 October 1890) and Starken-
burg (25 January 1894). A concise and constructive analysis
of the development of the conception of determination in the
works of Marx and Engels is offered by Hall (1977). The focus
of my discussion will fall upon two contrasting interpretations
of, and solutions to, the problem of determination within Marxist
analysis, namely those to be found in the works of Williams,
whose approach in some respects parallels that of Thompson,
and Althusser respectively.

Generally the problem of determination within Marxism has
been conceptualised in terms of a relationship between 'the
economic structure of society, the real foundation' and that
which has been assumed to be dependent upon it, namely an
'immense superstructure'. Williams, in a series of clarifications
and constructively critical analyses of the 'base-and-super-
structure' metaphor, as it was expressed in the 1859 Preface
and as it has been subsequently interpreted, has argued that

> In the transition from Marx to Marxism ... the words used
> in the original arguments were projected, first, as if they
> were precise concepts, and second, as if they were descrip-
> tive terms for observable 'areas' of social life. (1977, p. 77)

The position advanced by Williams is that the terms were ori-
ginally relational but that this original sense was overlaid by
interpretations of the terms as either 'relatively enclosed categories' or 'relatively enclosed areas of activity'. This translation
of the terms in turn made a further development possible, namely
the attribution of a temporal or spatial dimension to the relationship, viz. 'first material production, then consciousness, then
politics and culture' (ibid., p. 78), or, underlying everything,
the base, economic production and then upon this 'infrastructure' the various visible secondary levels of the superstructure.

Williams has commented that those formal abstract categories of
'base' and 'superstructure', have in fact become an obstruction
to analysis, for they have displaced real human activities and
historical processes as the object of study. Thus Williams has
proposed that the relationship of determination needs to be
explored, not in terms of the conceptions of 'the base' and 'the
superstructure' which signify concrete areas or objects, but
rather within 'indissoluble real processes'. Indeed, not only
has Williams observed that the complexity of real relations may
not be satisfactorily grasped in terms of a relationship between
base and superstructure but, furthermore, he has argued that
the translation of these metaphors into abstract categories or
concrete areas is at the root of the problem of determination.

Although Williams has stated that Marxism would be worthless
without a concept of determination, he has simultaneously
argued that it is 'radically disabled' by many of its existing
conceptions. In attempting to resolve the problem of the relationship of determination at the heart of Marxist analysis Williams
has drawn a distinction between two senses in which the concept
has been employed. First, the concept has been employed with
reference to objective circumstances or laws which have conditioned or regulated the course of social events. The implication
here is that people are subject to, or determined by, conditions
over which they may have no control or influence. Thus within
economistic forms of Marxism an emphasis has been placed upon
the inexorable laws of the economy and their determination of
social and historical processes independently of the will of
human agents. This conception of the determining process as,
in an absolute sense, beyond the control of human agents should
be contrasted with an alternative conception of determination
which restores 'the idea of direct agency'.

The second sense in which determination has been employed
has been with reference to the limits within which 'we make our
history'. In this instance determination is conceptualised in
terms of social and historical processes rather than in terms of
quasi-natural laws, thus the objective conditions into which
people are born are conceptualised as limits within which human
agency may be exercised. However, Williams has argued that
there is a danger, even with this second conception of determination as the setting of limits through social and historical
processes, 'of falling back into a new passive and objectivist
model' (ibid., p. 86), namely one in which a conception of 'the
objectified general process', that is to say society, may be constituted as the powerful determining force to which individuals
are subject. This is the context in which Williams has briefly
outlined a solution to the problem of determination within
Marxism.

The conception of determination as the setting of limits has
been described by Williams as partial or incomplete. Instead he
has proposed a 'full concept of determination', one which might
embrace both positive and negative determinations, 'the exertion

of pressures' as well as the setting of limits. The complex relations between these positive and negative determinations are
located within what has been described as 'the whole social
process', by which Williams seems to mean society as a dynamic
constitutive process. The advantages of Williams's formulation
are clear: it avoids the pitfalls of the conception of determination in terms of quasi-natural laws, it overcomes the negativity
of the 'setting of limits' conception of determination, and in
addition it reintroduces human activity into the process of
determination. What are we left with, however?

Williams has situated relations of domination within the whole
social process rather than between a particular abstracted element or structure and all other structures. In this way he has
avoided the conception of objectified autonomous structures as
the locus of determination and has been able to place an emphasis upon the importance of human activity, consciousness, and
experience in the making of history. The difficulty with this
formulation is that the concept of the whole social process is
lacking in clarity. The concept seems to represent the complex
constitutive process within which the present is continually
produced and re-produced. Therefore it encompasses all the
complex relations from which history is made, from 'political,
social and economic formations' to forms of social action and
individual experience. As such the concept permits no residue
or remainder, it is synonymous with the totality. We might note
that Williams has encountered a similar difficulty in his discussion of the concepts of production and productive forces. In this
instance the reference, which has predominated within Marxism,
to production as essentially 'economic' is replaced by a focus
on the 'production and reproduction of real life' to which all
and any activities in the social process as a whole may contribute (ibid., pp. 90-4). In conclusion, we might note that whilst
attempting to relieve Marxism of disabling conceptions of determination, Williams may have inadvertently dissolved the specificity of Marxist analysis.

OVERDETERMINATION AND RELATIVE AUTONOMY

Another approach to the problem of determination may be found
in the work of Althusser. For Althusser determination is conceptualised as a relationship between 'practices' or 'levels'
located within a social formation rather than in terms of a relationship between 'the base' and 'the superstructure'. To understand Althusser's analysis of determination it is therefore
necessary to briefly consider his conceptualisation of the different practices of which the social formation is composed.

Althusser has argued that the social formation is composed of
'different specific *levels of human practice* (economic practice,
political practice, ideological practice, scientific practice)' (1969,
p. 222). Furthermore, all these levels have their own 'charac-

teristic articulations', specificity and dynamic, which are based, in turn, upon 'the specific articulations of the unity of human society' (ibid.). In addition, each of the levels of the social formation has its own contradictions, and the accumulation of these respectively different contradictions may, at a specific historical moment, produce a radical transformation. Now, such a historical moment is a complex product and may not therefore be explained simply in terms of economic determination. The respective levels or practices which make up a social formation are, at any one moment, in a complex structured relationship within which another level or practice than the economic may be dominant.

However, the significant qualification inserted by Althusser is that it is the economic level or practice which ultimately determines which of the levels is to be dominant. Thus, a revolutionary transformation will not be the product of a simple form of economic determination emanating from a contradiction within the economic level between the forces and social relations of production, but will be the effect of an accumulation of different contradictions specific to each level of the social formation, expressed through the dominance of one of the levels which, in turn, will have achieved its dominance through the determining role of the economic level, in-the-final-instance.

Althusser has employed the concept of overdetermination to theorise the effects of the contradictions internal to each level or practice in the social formation, on the social formation as a whole, on each respective level, and on each of their respective contradictions. Nevertheless, although determination assumes the form of a complex interrelationship of levels and their effects within a structured whole or unity, it is the economic level or practice which remains the ultimate determinant. The other concept which Althusser has introduced to theorise the relationship of determination between the respective levels or practices within the social formation is that of relative autonomy, a concept which is the necessary complement to that of overdetermination. Althusser has argued that each of the various levels or positions within the social formation has its own specific effectivity, in other words that they are each 'relatively autonomous' from the other levels. Thus the problem of determination is reformulated. We may on the one hand retain a conception of 'determination in the last instance by the [economic] mode of production', but on the other hand we now have a conception of 'the relative autonomy of the superstructures and their specific effectivity' (ibid., p. 111).

For Althusser the elements of a more complex conception of determination are already present in the works of Marx and Engels, in particular in the correspondence of the latter with Bloch (cf. Feuer, 1971, pp. 436-9). In this text Althusser has identified the 'two ends of the chain' of determination: 'the economy is determinant, but *in the last instance*, Engels is prepared to say, in the long run, the run of History. But

History "asserts itself" through the multiform world of the superstructures' (Althusser, 1969, p. 112). The implication drawn from this by Althusser is that there can be no simple contradictions in any circumstances. Contradictions are not merely overdetermined in 'unique and aberrant historical situations', they are always overdetermined. Determination is not vested solely in the economic level, for effective determinations are derived from the other levels of the social formation (the superstructures), which in turn are accredited with a degree of relative autonomy. However, although Althusser may have challenged the sovereignty of 'His Majesty the Economy' by employing the concepts of overdetermination and relative autonomy in his reformulation of the relationship of determination within Marxism, he nevertheless retains a conception of economic determination-in-the-final-instance. Indeed, the retention of this premise, ambiguous though it might seem in the above context, may be regarded as an inevitable consequence of Althusser's particular reading of Marx and preoccupation with the question of a scientific analysis of modes of production.

Althusser's analysis of determination in terms of the presence of complex relationships between relatively autonomous levels of the social formation and the social formation itself, has met with several criticisms. There are three particular criticisms which I would like to note here, namely those advanced by Williams (1977), Thompson (1978), and Hindess (1977), respectively. Williams has briefly argued that, whilst the concept of overdetermination introduced by Althusser may allow us to understand 'historically lived situations and the authentic complexities of practice' (1977, p. 88), it may also, as is the case with the concept of determination, precipitate a neglect of the real locus of all practice, namely human activity. The fear expressed by Williams is that all human activity and lived experience may be subsumed within a 'categorial objectification of overdetermined structures'. Thompson's objections are comparable to those of Williams, although more detailed and sustained. Amongst a series of criticisms advanced by Thompson the following comments are especially relevant here. First, Althusser is criticised for failing to interrogate the concepts of determination and relative autonomy, for neglecting to show us how we might put such concepts to work. Second, the analysis of the social formation in terms of levels is subjected to criticism, in particular because it signifies the eviction of human agency. Thus, for Thompson

Althusser's constructions are actively *wrong* and thoroughly misleading. His notion of 'levels' motoring around in history at different speeds and on different schedules is an academic fiction. For all these 'instances' and 'levels' are in fact human activities, institutions and ideas. (1978, p. 289)

The final criticism to be noted here is perhaps of greater
significance in so far as it is derived from the work of one of
Althusser's former fellow-travellers, namely Hindess. Hindess
has argued that there seems to be an insurmountable contradiction between the conception of determination by the economy
and that of the relative autonomy of other levels or practices.
The concept of relative autonomy 'illustrates the contradiction
perfectly by affirming that while political and cultural relations
are autonomous from the economy they are only relatively so'
(1977, pp. 98-9). Hindess has explored the significance of this
contradiction in the field of Marxist analyses of classes and
politics. Essentially the problem is whether it is possible to
reconcile a conception of social classes, class relations and political forces defined in terms of a particular determinate relationship to the mode of production, that is to say classes as economic, political and ideological unities where the former is determinate, with another conception prevalent within Marxist
analysis, namely that political forces and ideological forms are
not effects of class (economic) determinations.

Consideration of the problem of the conception of social classes and politics within Marxism has led Hindess to conclude that

> *Either* we effectively reduce political and ideological pheno-
> mena to class interests determined elsewhere (basically in
> the economy) - i.e. an economic reductionism coupled with
> a vague recognition that things are actually more complicated
> and a failure to get to grips with that complication. *Or* we
> must face up to the real autonomy of political and ideological
> phenomena and their irreducibility to manifestations of inter-
> ests determined by the structure of the economy. (Ibid.,
> p. 104)

In other words, either we have basically economistic forms of
analysis in which politics is reduced to class interests or we
have to analyse power relations and political forces without
prejudice. A possible implication of the latter is that such analyses may extend beyond the limits of a Marxist problematic.

It is difficult not to reach the conclusion that particular theoretical problems, which have been a consistent feature of the
Marxist tradition, have defied resolution. At best they may
have been clarified, yet their very persistence is indicative of
a possible insolubility within the existing terms of reference.
For example, the question of the epistemological status of Marxist analysis seems to have become a persistent problem, a
perennial source of controversy amongst Marxists. With the
realisation of particular limitations, gaps or absences in the
classical tradition this issue has preoccupied generations of
Marxist theorists (cf. Anderson, 1976). Furthermore, the various associated forms of analysis have not only failed to resolve
this question but, in addition, they have been identified as the
principal source from which damaging analyses of the social

process, and thereby of politics and political practice, have been generated. For example, it has been argued by theorists with significantly different orientations to the Marxist tradition that the conception of Marxism as a science may be associated with the production of a form of knowledge which goes hand in hand with the development of systems of technical control and bureaucratically organised forms of administration. A preoccupation with the confirmation of the scientificity of Marxism has been identified as the source of the neglect of the centrality of human agency, experience, and consciousness within the social process and as responsible for the erosion of another dimension to be found in Marx's work, namely that tradition of critical analysis which has been regarded as necessary to the project for the realisation of human emancipation (cf. Habermas, 1974; Thompson, 1978).

The other problem of Marxist theory to which I have given some consideration is that of determination. This has proved to be equally difficult to resolve and to be of comparable significance for Marxist analyses of politics. The problem of determination, like that of the epistemological status of historical materialism, has been inherited from the classical Marxist tradition. In the works of Marx and Engels it is clear that the economy is determinant in-the-final-instance and therefore that the superstructures are in some sense determined. However, the latter are accorded some degree of effectivity which is not simply reducible to the economy. The problem has arisen from the fact that the link between these 'two ends of the chain' has yet to be forged. One of the most serious consequences of the lack of any precise mechanism connecting these two propositions – economic determination and the relative autonomy of the superstructures – has been the absence of a theory of the political level. As Stedman Jones has succinctly observed:

> The absence, on the theoretical plane, of any mechanism to connect the determination in the last instance by the economy and the relative autonomy of superstructures, was reproduced on the political plane in an inability to produce a systematic theory of revolutionary politics. (1973, p. 35)

The implication of my earlier comments is that the continuing absence of such a mechanism will remain a feature of Marxist analysis, for the two propositions are irreconcilable. Therefore, either analyses of politics and power will continue to be little more than more or less sophisticated forms of economism, or politics and power will be theorised autonomously of the economy. Whether a non-economistic analysis of politics may be generated from within a Marxist problematic remains a matter of conjecture.

The problems of Marxist theory extend beyond the particular issues discussed here. For example, we might refer to the continuing absence of any developed analysis of the capitalist state, the neglect of nation states and the revival of nationalism, and

the lack of analyses of the societies of actually existing socialism
and of comparisons with the capitalist societies of Western
Europe. In addition to omissions or gaps within Marxist theory
there is, of course, the question of the continuing relevance,
or obsolescence, of particular concepts and theories, for example, the concept of the dictatorship of the proletariat, the
theory of surplus value as a general theory of exploitation, and
the thesis of class polarisation (cf. Anderson, 1976). However,
of all the problems encountered within Marxist theory, the question of its 'truth-value', its scientificity or epistemological status,
has been paramount, as has been the premise which has constituted the specificity of Marxism, namely that of determination-
in-the-final-instance. We should perhaps consider the possibility
that the persistence of these and other problems points to the
limits, or even the limitations, of Marxist analysis, remembering
all the while that the strength of an analysis and its method is
derived from a recognition of its limits.

2 MARXISM, THEORY AND POLITICS

If the recent history of Marxism, particularly the tradition of Western Marxism, has revealed a disproportionate preoccupation with philosophical and epistemological questions, it is not so much indicative of a complete neglect of political conceptions and ideas as it is a reflection or consequence of the evident limitations of the conceptions and analyses formulated by Marx and Engels for an understanding of politics and power. Behind the significance and priority accorded to the philosophical and epistemological dimension in Marxist analysis there is the problem of political analysis and strategy, the crisis of Marxist political movements, parties and nation states with political systems 'modelled' on Marxist or Marxist-Leninist principles. Indeed, it is through the increasing crisis of Marxist politics that we may reach an understanding of the preoccupation with Marxist theory, its fundamental premises, concepts and epistemological grounds – a preoccupation which seems to have taken the form either of a search for solutions to the problems of political analysis and strategy, or of a retreat from such concerns. In this chapter I will focus on the political dimension of the crisis of Marxism.

The works of Marx and Engels clearly had a firm political foundation. Even if we were to agree with Althusser that the most significant feature of the work of Marx was that he '"opened up" for scientific knowledge a new "continent", that of *history'* (1969, p. 14), it would be difficult not to recognise that his work might also be regarded as the principal source of the theory of proletarian revolutions, and that the latter constitutes an important part of its continuing relevance and significance. Indeed, if we may differentiate between texts written explicitly as interventions in the politics of the labour movement and other texts which represent attempts to constitute a scientific basis for social analysis, we should perhaps remember that it is principally a matter of emphasis and focus that distinguishes the respective texts. The problems associated with the conceptions of politics and power to be found in the works of Marx and Engels have continually been interpreted as signs of the incompletion of their analyses, rather than as possible indicators of the necessary limits of their problematic. In consequence, the quest for an 'internal' solution to the problem of politics and power has been a consistent feature on the agenda of Marxist analysis.

THE CRISIS OF POLITICS

From its inception Marxism has claimed an association with scientificity and has sought to distance itself from moral or utopian
forms of socialist theory. People may not make the world just
as they please, for possibilities for change are limited and
shaped by material circumstances and conditions. To transform
the world a knowledge of the limiting material conditions is
vital. The implication of this position is that the world is to some
extent programmable, that through the knowledge produced by
Marxist analysis and implemented in political practice a rational
ordering of the social world may be possible. In other words,
a new social order may be engineered through an understanding
of the 'laws' of social and historical processes, coupled with
the struggle of progressive social forces against the inertia and
resistance of the existing order. It is not a matter of the greater
moral value of communism, as compared to capitalism, that
authorises the politics of the progressive forces, but rather
that the former, communism, lies in wait for humanity as the
(only) alternative to the barbarity into which capitalism is
doomed to degenerate. At the heart of Marxist analysis there
has been an assumption of a scientific conception of social development, within which a sparsely formulated conception of
socialism has constituted the transitional stage of development
between capitalism and the achievement of a higher social formation, namely communism. This is the context in which the October Revolution in Russia, made by Lenin in the name of Marxism,
became such a significant event for Marxist politics. The close
association of the new social order, which emerged from the
revolution, with the concept of the transitional stage of socialism formulated within Marxist theory provided the model of
socialism. In the absence of any detailed articulation of the concept of socialism Marxists have tended to regard Soviet society
as demonstrating, with all its teething problems, the possibility
of socialism. However, this model of socialism can no longer be
sustained, for a series of events have precipitated a fundamental re-examination of the conception of socialism and of Marxist
political analysis and strategy.
   It might be argued that an alternative tradition which has
developed from the works of Marx has successfully evaded the
problems associated with 'official' Marxism. I am thinking in
particular of analyses which have emphasised either the creative
and constructive potential of human agency, consciousness and
experience in contrast to forms of structural determination
revealed through scientific analysis, or the possible emancipatory benefits of critical theorising and analysis in contrast to
the dehumanising effects of rational scientific inquiry (cf.
Thompson, 1978; Habermas, 1972, 1974). However, in such
cases a parallel and related set of problems have emerged concerning the grounds of analysis, the implications for political
analysis and strategy, and finally a general absence of discus-

sion of any implied possible alternative social formation. One
further observation which might be made of such analyses is
that their relationship to, and location within, the Marxist tradition may itself be regarded as a matter of controversy, in so
far as they have abandoned the central concepts of classical
Marxism (cf. Callinicos, 1982, p. 21).

The realisation that there is no longer a model for socialism
may not have resolved any problems, but it has at least provided a context within which a more open recognition of the
limitations of Marxism has become possible. Ultimately the limitations identified reduce to two fundamental issues, namely that
Marxism lacks a theory of politics and, in addition, has no solution to the problem of power. The specific limitations and problems identified are to be found within both classical Marxism
and Western Marxism. For example, we might note that Marx did
not produce any 'coherent or comparative analysis of the political structures of bourgeois class power' (cf. Anderson, 1976,
p. 114); neglected the development of the state and changes in
the international state system; did not appreciate the importance
of nationalism and national cultures; and generated within
'Capital' a merely regional theory of exploitation which, because
it has subsequently been employed as a complete theory, has
contributed to the division between, and subordination of,
political struggle to economic struggle. Problems of a comparable
significance may be found in Lenin's work. For example, Anderson has pointed to the contradiction between Lenin's conception
of 'soviet democratism', workers' councils as the necessary
revolutionary form of proletarian power, and the subsequent
reality of party authoritarianism and the development of a monolithic bureaucratic apparatus. Indeed, he has suggested that
the latter development was in part a consequence of Lenin's
failure to link or integrate 'his doctrine of the party with his
account of the soviets' (ibid., p. 116). Furthermore, the works
of both Marx and Lenin reveal a conception of the inevitable
decline and transcendence of capitalism, and this in turn obvi-
ated the need for any development of a theory of politics in their
respective writings.

There are, of course, other classical Marxist theorists and in
addition other absences, ambiguities, and misconceptions which
have been transmitted to contemporary Marxist analysis. However, my concern is less with the origin of a particular problem
in the work of a founding father than with the limitations of
contemporary Marxism and the scope for solutions to the problem of politics and power. In his critical analysis of contemporary
Marxism, Anderson has documented several questions which
have remained unanswered, questions which concern critical
economic and political realities. These range from the nature and
structure of bourgeois democracy and appropriate forms of
political strategy in Western democratic states, to 'the contemporary laws of motion of capitalism as a mode of production'.
Many of the questions identified by Anderson have been the

focus of a common concern throughout the many schools of
Marxist thought, although the solutions which have been
generated have varied enormously (cf. Blackburn, 1977; Miliband, 1977; Althusser, 1978b; Altvater and Kallscheuer, 1979).
Thus, even if all Marxists have not joined Althusser's celebration of the open recognition of a crisis of Marxism as a progressive development, it is evident that there is a broad agreement
over the existence of fundamental limitations in Marxist political
analysis.

The general absence of any systematic theorising of politics
and power in classical Marxism is reflected within contemporary
Marxist thought in a preoccupation with the problem of the state.
It is worth emphasising that the assumption has persisted that
politics and power may be adequately conceptualised within a
Marxist analytic framework; in other words, that from within an
analysis of the capitalist mode of production, located broadly
within the discourse of political economy, it remains possible to
generate appropriate concepts of politics and power, conceptions
that will extend and develop our understanding of contemporary
societies. Generally the form such analyses have taken has
been that of an attempt to develop an analysis of the state in
Western capitalist societies. The state has thus been identified
as the locus of political power and in consequence other forms
of politics and power have been neglected.

POWER, POLITICS AND THE STATE

Contemporary Marxist analyses of the state have taken various
forms, encompassing on the one hand the general position that
it is possible to derive an analysis of the state as a political form
from the dynamics of the capitalist mode of production, for
example the several contributions to the 'state derivation'
debate (cf. Holloway and Picciotto, 1978), and on the other
hand analyses which seek to establish the 'relative autonomy'
of the political (cf. Althusser, 1971; Poulantzas, 1973; Miliband,
1977). Both of these positions should be distinguished from
economistic analyses which seek to formulate a theory of the
state in terms of the requirements of capital and thereby neglect
completely the specificity of the political (cf. Yaffe and Bullock,
1975).

Although 'state derivationist' analyses have distinguished
between the economic and the political level, an understanding
of the distinctiveness of these respective levels has been generated from an analysis of the nature of capitalist production.
Basically there have been three contributions to the state derivation debate. Common to each of these contributions is the
view that Marx's 'Capital' may provide the basis from which an
understanding of political forms in bourgois society may be
constructed. It is not a matter for the 'derivationists' of returning to the base-superstructure metaphor in order to understand

the relation between the economic and the political, but rather
of asking, 'What is it about social relations in bourgeois society
that makes them appear in separate forms as economic relations
and political relations?' (Holloway and Picciotto, 1978, p. 18).
I will briefly note the different approaches to the analysis of
the form of the capitalist state presented within the 'state
derivation' debate.

In the first approach the existence of the state as a separate
institution is accounted for in terms of the form of the relations
between capitals. An autonomous state is conceptualised as
standing above the competition between individual capitals and
as necessary for the reproduction of the conditions of capitalist
production as a whole. Thus the state is conceptualised as a
regulating mechanism, independent of the relations of commodity
production, performing specific general functions necessary
for total social capital. In the second approach the apparent
neutrality of the state is the focus of analysis. The key issue
here is the nature of the process by which the state, a form of
class rule, achieves a degree of neutrality and thus a measure
of acceptance by the working class. An explanation of this
'neutral' state is derived from an analysis of the forms of
appearance of capitalist relations on the surface of society,
rather than from the underlying structure of class relations.
Thus the apparently neutral state is represented as a product
of a superficial community of interest amongst all the (revenue-
owning) members of a capitalist society. The third approach
has sought to derive an analysis of the form of the state from
the nature of the social relations of exploitation and domination.
Thus, rather than represent the state as operating in the
general interest of capital, a feature common to both of the
other approaches, it has placed emphasis upon the coercive,
class character of the state. However, 'the state is not presented crudely as an instrument of class rule but as a specific
and historically conditioned form of the social relations of
exploitation' (Holloway and Picciotto, 1978, p. 24).

The 'state derivation' form of analysis is very much a product,
as Altvater and Kallscheuer have noted, of the particular circumstances of Marxist culture within the Federal Republic of
Germany, namely the product of a predominantly 'free-floating'
academic Left which has lacked the reference or support of a
strong workers' movement. It thus constitutes an analysis
produced purely from within an opposition culture, and in
consequence there is an absence of, and no perceived need for,
a positive conception of politics. Furthermore, although 'state
derivation' analyses may have provided a degree of understanding of the limits of the welfare state, of state action and intervention, their conclusions are ultimately predicated on the logic
of 'Capital' and therefore vulnerable to criticism. In attempting
to derive an analysis of the state from the dynamics of the
capitalist mode of production, from an analysis of the economic
reproduction of bourgeois society, the 'state derivation'

approach is unable to account for the fact that

> bourgeois rule does not 'collapse' with economic crisis, ...
> that there are necessarily domains, institutions, relation-
> ships and mechanisms in bourgeois societies which produce
> a social hegemony of the bourgeois class going beyond the
> securing of its rule that results from economic reproduction.
> (Altvater and Kallscheuer, 1979, pp. 103-4)

An alternative to the economistic state derivation approaches
is an analysis of the state and politics as relatively autonomous.
The starting point for such an analysis has been, as I have
already noted, the texts in which Marx and Engels sought to
formulate their conception of the determinative mode of
production. A significant difference between the 'relative autonomy' and 'state derivation' approaches is that in the former
there is no a priori assumption that an analysis of power, politics and the state may be generated from the logic of 'Capital'.
However, notwithstanding such an important difference, there
are similarities, namely a common assumption of the possibility
of a Marxist theory of power, politics, and the state and a common tendency to conflate the exercise of power with the apparatus of the state.
I do not propose to pursue the various stages of the debate
over the conception of the relative autonomy of the levels of the
superstructure. It will suffice here to note that since Althusser
(1969) derived the conception from Engels's qualificatory comments on the pitfalls of historical materialism it has been widely
recognised as providing the basis of a significant advance in
Marxist analyses of politics, allowing the economic and the political to be conceptualised as relatively autonomous instances.
More recently the status of the concept of relative autonomy as
a solution to the equally undesirable alternatives of, on the one
hand, an untenable economic reductionism and, on the other
hand, a non-Marxist conception of the unqualified autonomy of
the various levels of the social formation, has met with considerable criticism (cf. Cutler et al., 1977, 1978; Thompson, 1978).
One line of criticism, exemplified by the work of Thompson, has
been that the concept of relative autonomy constitutes nothing
more than a 'warning-notice'. It reminds us of the perils of
reductionism but tells us virtually nothing about the conditions
of existence of the different formations and levels of society.
In short the concept is no substitute for detailed historical
analysis. The other main line of criticism, exemplified by the
work of Cutler et al., has been that an understanding of superstructural practices or levels may not be simply 'read off' from
an analysis of the mode of production, that conceptions of politics and ideology may not be derived from the economy, or from
class interests. A brief statement of this second line of criticism
of the concept of relative autonomy is present in the work of
Hindess (1977), to which I have already made reference.

Hindess has suggested that there is a degree of ambiguity surrounding conceptions of social class and class relations in Marxism. Classes are conceptualised both in terms of determinate relations of production, that is to say in economic terms, as economic agents, and in addition as social subjects engaged in political and ideological struggle. This ambiguity may be resolved either by employing a reductionist formulation of the unity of social class, determined in the economy, or, treating the conception of autonomy seriously, we might conclude that there is no necessary economic, political and ideological unity and that political forces may not be deduced from, and are not tied to, class relations determined in the economy. The former position returns us to a familiar if barren terrain, namely to the treatment of political strategy in terms of the interests of social classes determined by the structure of the economy. The latter position, of the irreducibility of political and ideological phenomena, leads to an altogether different formulation, one which displaces the conventional terms of reference embodied in the 'base-superstructure' metaphor. Thus Hindess has proposed that the social formation be conceptualised as a 'social form in which the conditions of existence of determinate relations of production are secured' (ibid., p. 99), but where relations of production do not determine either the forms of other relations or the forms of their own conditions of existence. In other words capitalist relations of production may have determinate political-legal and ideological-cultural conditions of existence, but they do not determine the particular form of those conditions; rather, these are subject to modification through the struggle of political forces which are not reducible to economic class interests. In this way conventional Marxist analyses of politics are displaced by proposals for the generation of a non-essentialist mode of analysis.

By way of a tentative summary we can distinguish between three approaches to the analysis of the political level: in the first the state and politics are theorised through an analysis of the conditions of economic reproduction of bourgeois society (e.g. economistic and materialist 'state derivation' approaches); in the second approach politics is constituted as a relatively autonomous level of the social formation subject to a process of (over)determination-in-the-final-instance by the economic (the structure in dominance within the capitalist mode of production); finally politics may be considered to be genuinely autonomous. The first two approaches may be readily subsumed within the history of Marxism; the final approach, the 'autonomy of the political', may well lie beyond the scope of Marxist theory. To pursue this a little further I will turn to the work of Gramsci and the conception of hegemony, for it is here that Marxists have sought to uncover the beginning of an analysis of politics and power freed from the limitations of economism and determination-in-the-final-instance.

It has generally been accepted that economism or economic

reductionist theories of politics and power constituted the central target of Gramsci's work. Whereas in the work of Marx and Engels an analysis of the superstructures is at best secondary to an analysis of the economic structure, in Gramsci's work the former constitutes the focus, hence the appellation 'theorist of the superstructures'. As with the work of the other classical thinkers in the Marxist tradition there are several versions of Gramsci's work. However, two contrasting interpretations of Gramsci's work have predominated. On the one hand his work has been represented as an inversion of Marxist orthodoxy in so far as it accords primacy to the superstructures over the economic structure, and to civil society, or the ideological moment (consensus, hegemony), over political society, or the institutional moment (domination, force) (cf. Bobbio, 1979b). On the other hand his work has been interpreted as fundamentally compatible with the theoretical problematic of Marx in so far as a common subscription to the principle of economic determination-in-the-final-instance is evident in their respective analyses (cf. Texier, 1979). At issue here is the question of the relationship of Gramsci's work to the fundamental premises and central themes of the Marxist tradition and the relevance of his development of a series of concepts (e.g. relations of force, hegemony, historical bloc) for Marxist analysis of politics.

In the work of Marx the state of the political order is conceptualised as subordinate to civil society, in which economic relations constitute the decisive element. In Gramsci's work the state, or political society, constitutes one of the two major superstructural levels, the other being civil society. Whereas for Marx the concept of civil society embraced 'the whole material intercourse of individuals within a definite stage of the development of productive forces' (1976b, p. 89), for Gramsci the concept refers to the whole of ideological-cultural relations, to spiritual and intellectual life (cf. Bobbio, 1979b, pp. 30-1). The difference between these two formulations is considerable. In the case of the formulation derived from Marx's work we are back to a position in which the state and politics are subordinated to the economic structure, conceptualised as an instrument of class domination. In Gramsci's work we encounter an analysis which directly addresses the problem of politics, not by reducing the phenomena of power and politics solely to the form of the state, and thence to the economy or the economic level, but rather through the introduction of a positive conception of civil society, which is constituted as the mediating moment between the economic structure and the coercive force of the state.

The key concept in Gramsci's analysis of civil society is that of hegemony. The concept addresses not only the subtlety, complexity, durability, and apparent acceptability of bourgeois class rule in Western Europe, but in addition indicates that the political strategy of the subordinate classes must begin with the transformation of civil society, with ideological struggle.

Gramsci's concept of hegemony refers to the process of intellectual and moral leadership through which consent is achieved
or won and it includes, as Bobbio has noted,

> both the moment of political leadership and the moment of
> cultural leadership. Therefore it embraces, as its own bear-
> ers, not only the party, but all the other institutions of
> civil society (in Gramsci's meaning of the term) which have
> some connection with the elaboration and diffusion of culture.
> (1979b, p. 40)

Hegemony is exercised, or consent is won, by means of and
through a network of cultural institutions including schools,
churches, the media, trades unions, political associations and
parties (cf. Gramsci, 1976, pp. 55-60).

Following Bobbio's interpretation we may identify two significant advances in Gramsci's work: first, the beginnings of a
non-reductionist analysis of politics and power, and, second,
a conceptualisation of these phenomena in terms other than the
form of the state as a political-juridical organisation. In Gramsci's work there seems to be a shift of emphasis from a conception of the institutional location of power in the form of the
state to a conception of the ideological moment at which hegemony is achieved, or as Bobbio has formulated it, institutions
are displaced by ideologies as the 'primary moment of history'
(1979b, pp. 35-6). Bobbio has attempted to demonstrate the
relevance of Gramsci's work for contemporary social analysis
and political strategy. Furthermore, he has argued that Gramsci's conceptual scheme constitutes a significant advance upon
that of Marx and that it is not subject to the limits and limitations of economism to which Marxist analysis is vulnerable.
However, Bobbio's version of the relationship between the works
of Marx and Gramsci respectively has been subjected to criticism.
Perhaps the most significant objection has been that the comparison of their respective works is undermined, first, by an
over-mechanistic interpretation of Marx's work and, second,
by the failure to consider Gramsci's endorsement of the primacy
of the 'infrastructure' or the economy (cf. Texier, 1979).

I do not propose to become embroiled in an interminable pursuit of the 'authentic' relationship of the 'essential' Gramsci to
the 'real' Marx. I merely wish to underline the existence of
a substantial difference of opinion over the nature and value of
Gramsci's work and its relationship to the central tenets of the
Marxist tradition, and to note that readings may be differentiated in terms of their respective commitments either to the
preservation of a strong link between Marx and Gramsci or to
an unprejudiced examination of the actual and possible relevance
of Gramsci's work for an alternative conceptualisation of politics
and power, which may ultimately fall outside the conventional
parameters of a Marxist analysis. A possible exception may be
found in Mouffe's (1979) attempt both to claim a special place

for Gramsci's work within the theoretical framework of Marxism
and to identify his work as the source of a radically different
conception of politics and power. Mouffe has argued that it is
possible to identify in Gramsci's work an embryonic solution
to the problem of the incompatibility of the conception of the
relative autonomy of the superstructures and the definitive
principle of historical materialism, namely determination in the
final instance by the economy. Specifically it is in Gramsci's
construction of an anti-reductionist, 'anti-economistic problematic of ideology' and politics that Mouffe has identified the
promise of a solution to the 'determination-autonomy' contradiction.

The designation of the problematic of hegemony as the space
within which it may be possible to show that there is no necessary incompatibility between a conception of the relative autonomy of the ideological superstructures and a conception of
economic determination remains a speculative feature of Mouffe's
reading of Gramsci; it constitutes work to be done. There is,
however, one other significant observation on Gramsci's conception of hegemony which promises to be more productive as
far as a non-reductionist analysis of politics and power is concerned. Mouffe has noted that Gramsci rejected the instrumental
conception of the state and politics inherent in the economism
of Marxism and conceptualised politics not as a separate, institutional practice, but as a 'dimension which is present in all
fields of human activity' (Mouffe, 1979, p. 201). In taking this
line, in recognising the presence in Gramsci's work of a non-
reductionist conception of politics, we vacate the theoretical
problematic of Marxism. This is implicitly acknowledged in
Mouffe's identification of a convergence between the logical
implications for research of Gramsci's non-reductionist problematic of hegemony and the conception of power it allows, namely that 'far from being localised in the repressive state apparatuses, power is exercised at all levels of society' (ibid., p. 201),
and the 'strategical' conception of power developed in the work
of Foucault (1977b, 1979a).

Mouffe's identification of a convergence between Gramsci's
thought and Foucault's genealogical analyses suggests at least
two interesting possibilities: either that quite substantial elements of Foucault's work are compatible with a Marxist analysis
(cf. Poulantzas, 1978), or that those particular dimensions of
Gramsci's work which converge with Foucault's analysis, and
which have been identified as the source of a possible solution
to central problems within Marxism, may constitute features
which transgress the conceptual limits of a Marxist analysis. If
we subscribe to the view that there is a fundamental compati-
bility between the theoretical problematics of Marx and Gramsci,
then the work of the latter cannot, in addition, constitute the
source of radical and 'external' solutions to the fundamental
theoretical and practical problems of Marxism. Inasmuch as
Gramsci's work embodies the central premises of Marxist analysis,

it follows that it must also share the general weaknesses and limitations associated with those premises. On the other hand, if we adopt the view that the work of Gramsci differs significantly from the mainstream Marxist tradition, then any solutions to the problems and limitations of that tradition derived from Gramsci's work may well extend beyond the conceptual limits of a Marxist analysis.

If we accept the view formulated by Hall, that the problematic developed by Foucault is at 'keypoints ... theoretically inconsistent with ... "classical Marxism"' (1980, p. 66), then one of the more significant implications of Mouffe's 'convergence thesis' seems to be that there is a considerable departure within Gramsci's work from the central tenets of Marxism. Thus the identification of Gramsci's work as the source from which possible alternative conceptions of politics and power may be generated, conceptions which are not subject to the limitations of conventional Marxist formulations, may simultaneously serve as an indirect confirmation of the limits of the Marxist problematic.

THE CONCEPT OF THE PARTY

The realisation that political forces may not simply be conceptualised as class-determined phenomena has had implications not only for Marxist conceptions of politics and power but also for the associated concept of the party. The emergence of new social subjects, the decline in membership, votes, and confidence in traditional working-class parties, and exchanges over possible alternatives to existing social policies, in particular the relative merits of the alternative strategies of reform and revolution, have each contributed to the controversy surrounding the concept of the party within Marxism. The roots of this contemporary controversy lie in ambiguities in the work of Marx and Engels.

Although it may be argued that the emphasis in the work of Marx and Engels was placed upon the spontaneity of working-class politics, or upon the self-emancipation of the working class, it is difficult to deny that a conception of a political vanguard may also be found in their work. For example, in the 'Manifesto of the Communist Party' we find reference being made to the relation between proletarians and communists in terms of the latter's practical and theoretical leadership of the working-class movement, a formulation which seems to presage Lenin's conception of the necessity of an organised political elite at the head of the movement for socialism. However, although we might identify elements of a conception of a vanguard in the work of Marx and Engels, it falls short of Lenin's conception of a vanguard party. Whereas for Lenin a socialist vanguard was deemed to be necessary if the working class was to be rescued from a domesticated preoccupation with the achievement of narrow economic gains through 'non-political' trade union activity, for Marx trade unions were conceptualised as political organisations. Indeed, in Marx's view the trade unions constituted 'schools of socialism' of far greater significance for the masses than any political party, and alone capable of 'representing a true working-class party' (cf. McLellan, 1971, p. 175).

My interest is not in saving Marx from Lenin, but rather in documenting the fact that, although Marx and Engels did not attach the same significance to the role of the party as did Lenin, they did nevertheless share a common conception of the necessity for a form of leadership to be exercised over the working class if they were to become an effective force for socialism. I do not propose to take the question of the relationship of Lenin's work to that of Marx and Engels any further at this stage, although, as we will see, it has assumed a considerable degree of importance for those who have engaged in the exercise of apportioning responsibility for the effects of Marxism (e.g. the 'Gulag question'). It will suffice to note that with Lenin's work there emerged an explicit conception of the party as the necessary organisational form of representation of working-class politics. Through the mechanism of a centralised socialist party, operating under the principles of a scientific Marxism, the working class was to be conveyed to its revolutionary destiny. We should take note that with the elevation of Marxist analysis to 'scientific socialism' it became evident that there would not be room for more than one party; there could only be one 'true' party of the working class.

Given the relatively pessimistic evaluation of the political potential of the working class, namely that left to their own devices they would eventually conspire to produce their own domestication, the inevitable corollary was the formulation of a conception of the necessity of the leading political and educational role of the Communist Party. Such a conception served to legitimate the emergence of a steadily increasing distance of authority and life-style, as well as differences in experience, qualification, and influence between the inner circle of the party and those whose interests it ostensibly represented. The misconception that scientific socialism was synonymous with the truth, and that the working class was a homogeneous social group with an underlying common interest, constituted the foundation on which single-party representation was predicated. The evaluation of the relative underdevelopment of the politics of the working class legitimated the construction of a centralised hierarchical authority, a bureaucratic party apparatus which was able to legislate in accordance with what it considered to be in the best long-term interests of the working class and consistent with a successful negotiation of the socialist transition to communism. The absence of any conception of 'postrevolutionary' politics in Marxism and the continuing ambiguity associated with the conception of socialism has allowed the rule of a political and bureaucratic elite, the dictatorship of one party, to be represented within Eastern Europe as a realisation of 'the dictatorship of the proletariat'.

The legacy of the October Revolution and scientific socialism
in its Marxist-Leninist form has cast a large shadow from which
contemporary radical social theory and politics has only relatively recently begun to emerge. With increasing recognition of
the atrophied character of the societies of 'actually existing
socialism' a critical process of re-examination has gathered
momentum, encompassing: the role of the party (e.g. Althusser,
1978b; Taylor, 1980); a reconsideration of the possible value
and desirability of such bourgeois institutions as freedom, democracy and pluralism; and analysis of the limitations of scientific
socialism and the concomitant necessity of a return to a form of
utopian thought (cf. Bahro, 1978, p. 253). One consequence of
this critical process of re-examination has been that several
Western European communist parties (e.g. PCI, PCE, CPGB)
have abandoned the conventional formulation of the necessity of
a dictatorship of the proletariat in the transitional phase of
socialism and replaced it with an alternative conception of a
democratic road to socialism. This shift from the concept of
'the dictatorship of the proletariat' to a concept of a democratic
road to socialism represents a movement away from a conception
of the party as the fount of all political wisdom, towards a
minimal recognition of other political movements, forces and
interests. It constitutes an acknowledgment of the necessity of
forming a qualitatively different relationship between political
organisations and the people if policies for fundamental social
change and reform are to have widespread support and a chance
of being fulfilled.

ON THE QUESTION OF SOCIALISM

The realisation that the societies of actually existing socialism
may no longer be regarded as satisfactory models of development
and transformation has produced an acute awareness of the
ambiguity of the conception of socialism at the heart of Marxist
theory and politics. The strengths of Marxist analysis have
conventionally rested with its possible provision of a scientific
mode of analysis and/or a global or totalising form of social
criticism. With the loss of credibility in evolutionary and pre-
dictive analyses of social development and the abandonment of
the idea of 'laws' of economic development, scientific Marxism
has been left with few resources from which to comment on either
the reality, or the possibility, of post-capitalist social formations. On the other hand, Marxism as a form of critique has at
best been able to offer a criticism of existing social conditions,
albeit embellished with speculative comments concerning the
possibilities latent within the human condition, derived from an
unexplicated philosophical anthropology. Either way Marxism
has, to date, had little of substance to offer on the nature of the
transition from capitalism to socialism and has provided possibly
even less comment on the nature and character of socialism

and/or communism.

The general absence of any sustained discussion of socialism, the first phase of communism, in the works of Marx and Engels seems to have been a measured response to the inadequacies associated with speculative and utopian forms of thought. Even in the 'Critique of the Gotha Programme', a text in which Marx directly confronted explicitly political issues and questions, it is evident that there was a general reluctance to speculate about the nature of socialism or communism in the absence of any knowledge of the requisite conditions of production. Rather, the work of Marx and Engels was directed towards an analysis and demonstration of the necessary disintegration of the capitalist mode of production and towards the establishment of a parallel political movement which would engender the abolition of capitalist private property. As they affirmed in 'The German Ideology':

> Communism is for us not a *state of affairs* which is to be established, an *ideal* to which reality [will] have to adjust itself. We call communism the *real* movement which abolishes the present state of things. (1976b, p. 49)

Similarly 'negative' sentiments may be found in the 'Manifesto of the Communist Party', where Marx and Engels make reference not only to the 'abolition of bourgeois property' but also to the related abolition of 'bourgeois individuality, bourgeois independence, and bourgeois freedom'. The cause in the name of which this abolition is sought may indeed be commendable, even desirable; however, the nature of that which is to emerge from the ruins of bourgeois society remains problematic and relatively unformulated. A highly relevant and sympathetic demonstration of the problematic nature of this issue is to be found in Bahro's (1978) analysis of the societies of actually existing socialism.

The focus of Bahro's work has fallen on what might be termed the increasing credibility gap in Eastern Europe, on the difference between the classical vision or promise of Marxism and the reality of actually existing socialism. It is a project which encompasses a brief examination of the sketches of socialism and communism in the classical texts, an analysis of the development and anatomy of the societies of Eastern Europe, and the construction of an ambitious programmatic statement concerning what Bahro has described as 'general emancipation' or human emancipation, for which a return to utopian thought appears to be a necessary prerequisite. I will confine my comments primarily to Bahro's observations on the classical vision and sketch of socialism which forms 'part of the *objective* preconditions ... involved in the revolutions of 1917 and after' (1978, p. 22).

For Marx the preconditions for socialism and communism materialised within capitalism; they were conceptualised as the product of the bourgeoisie's constantly necessary revolutionising

of the means of production. In proceeding with the view that a
theoretical foundation for the communist movement might lie in
the economic anatomy of capitalism, that communism might be
equated with the abolition of private property, Marx was already
committed to a position from which it would be exceedingly difficult, if not impossible, to anticipate the problems of politics,
the state, and power, and to countenance the possibility of
other, 'non-capitalist', roads to socialism. Because Marx placed
all the emphasis in his conception of communism on the abolition
of private property and such interconnected processes as

  (i)   the immediate socialisation of the means and conditions of
        production
 (ii)   the abolition of the traditional division of labour
(iii)   the appropriation of the means of production by the
        associated producers
 (iv)   the eventual abolition of the capitalist world market

he was unable to recognise that the transitional period of socialism, the period of the dictatorship of the proletariat, might
produce an indissoluble monolithic state machine (cf. Bahro,
1978, pp. 29-30). It is now quite clear that the power and
pervasiveness of the 'state machine' has created a situation in
which, even given the abolition of capitalist private property,
the producers do not exercise control over the processes of
production and distribution, but rather control is centralised,
hierarchically organised, and exercised by an elite, ostensibly
in the interests of the producers. This development is difficult to reconcile with several of Marx's comments on socialism
and communism.

For example, in 'The Civil War in France' Marx and Engels
made reference to the Paris Commune in terms which warned of
the dangers of the state and of the need to abolish 'the oppres-
sing power of the former centralised government, army, political
police, bureaucracy, which Napoleon had created in 1798 and
which since then had been taken over by every new government
as a welcome instrument and used against its opponents' (Feuer,
1971, p. 399). They advised that the working class should
'safeguard itself against its own deputies and officials' (ibid.,
p. 400) and that through the 'communal constitution' it would
be possible to restore 'to the social body all the forces hitherto
absorbed by the state parasite feeding upon, and clogging the
free movement of, society' (ibid., p. 408). For Marx and Engels
the commune seemed to represent the political form necessary
for establishing the economic emancipation of labour; it represented the dictatorship of the proletariat.

Bahro has observed that such critical and perceptive comments
by Marx and Engels on the state form are paralleled by, on the
one hand, an apparent unawareness of the possible positive
'economic organisational' and 'cultural-educational' functions of
the state apparatus and, on the other hand, by an inability to

anticipate that 'the unification of philosophy and the proletariat, of socialism (as science) and the workers' movement, would turn out very similar, after the revolution, to the earlier case of the third estate, from which the bourgeoisie came to power' (Bahro, 1978, p. 42). There was therefore not only an under-estimation or lack of consideration of the creative significance of the state in their work, but in addition no recognition of the possibility that the revolution would produce a new privileged scientific-political class, a new state apparatus which would not wither away. Bahro has suggested that with hindsight it is possible to 'perceive behind the authority of Marx and his doc-trine ... the shadow of Stalin' (ibid., p. 41), and to anticipate that the equation of communism with the abolition of private property and the transformation of the capitalist mode of pro-duction would produce a neglect of politics, power, and the state, and a consequential naivety about the nature of, and the problems likely to be encountered in, the transitional stage of socialism.

There has been, and to a considerable extent there remains, a tendency to gloss over the question of socialism. It is far easier to provide telling (and necessary) criticisms of the exist-ing social order, to indulge in critique or to offer proposals for reform, than it is to attempt to formulate dimensions of a pos-sible alternative social order. This has become even more evident with the loss of a credible model for socialism. Whereas it may once have been possible to invoke the USSR, China, or another society of actually existing socialism to demonstrate the realisa-tion of possibility, it is now a matter of recognising the exist-ence of significant differences between such societies and Marx's socialist theory, and of beginning to analyse the 'non-capitalist road' taken by the nominally socialist countries. For Bahro this has involved an analysis of the non-capitalist development of industrialisation in the societies of actually existing socialism in terms of 'the legacy of the so-called Asiatic mode of produc-tion'. The October Revolution is thus reconceptualised as 'the first *anti-imperialist revolution* in what was still a *predominantly pre-capitalist country*' (ibid., p. 50), and the emergence of new relations of domination, embodied in the state machine, is accounted for not in terms of the installation of a transitional stage of the dictatorship of the proletariat, but rather as having been historically necessary for the economic advancement of the USSR. Bahro has argued that, given the massive task of re-structuring the economy and of hastening the process of indus-trialisation, the construction of a bureaucratic state apparatus was unavoidable. For 'Without the apparatus of force that the Bolsheviks set in motion, Russia today would still be a peasant country, most probably on the capitalist road' (ibid., p. 101). Speculative as this might be, it does serve to underline Bahro's conception of the historical necessity of a strong centralised state apparatus for the production of 'capitalist work habits, discipline, and skill' in the labour force in the USSR during the period of early industrialisation. However, even if we accept the necessity of a strong state for the achievement of rapid industrialisation in pre-capitalist and post-revolution Russia, it is now evident that the institutionalisation of a dictatorship over the proletariat has become counter-productive for the development of socialism. At best the existing political system promises to deliver further economic developments and benefits; however, given the current economic crisis of Comecon, such promises appear extremely fragile (cf. Brus et. al., 1982). Furthermore, the promise and achievement of economic advance has increasingly assumed the form of a palliative for the perpetuation of existing relations of domination. Bureaucratic centralism thus constitutes the price for the existing level of economic rewards and (possible) future benefits.

A series of legitimations have been presented to account for the existence of monolithic state apparatuses in the societies of actually existing socialism. These have assumed the following general forms: political, whereby the rule of the party-state has been presented as representative of the people, as constituting the dictatorship of the proletariat; economic, whereby the state machine has been credited with the successful achievement of a programme of rapid industrialisation, which has transformed and improved the material well-being of the people; ideological, whereby the existing state form and programme for social development has been presented as a product of, and in accord with, the practice of scientific socialism. The collapse of each of these respective legitimations, coupled with the belief that

the only theory that is fit for penetrating the jungle of bureaucratic centralism and its politbureaucratic holy of holies, i.e. revolutionary Marxism, has been so effectively usurped by the party bureaucracy, by the apparatus's total power of disposal over the means of mass communication and education, that it meets with the general mistrust of the masses (ibid., p. 248),

has led Bahro to conclude that the formulation of a programme for 'general emancipation' now requires the adoption of a form of utopian thought.

Thus Bahro has expressed criticism both of the ideological appropriation of Marxism by the state in Eastern Europe and of the conception at the heart of 'scientific socialism' that scientific and technological progress may resolve mankind's social problems. His criticisms constitute an endorsement of Marcuse's (1971) critical analysis of Marxist theory as the rationality of the Soviet system and of the general line taken by the Frankfurt School on the forms of oppression and domination associated with instrumental reason. Bahro has proceeded from this analysis and critique of the societies of actually existing socialism to outline a conception of an alternative strategy, a programme for 'general emancipation'. Essentially, Bahro's position is that

the Eastern European societies have not emancipated people;
individuals are still subject to 'socially determined limitations
on their development' (1978, p. 255). To achieve human emancipation a radical transformation will be required, a 'cultural
revolution' in which the question of the organisation of the
'social whole' will be the focus of attention and activity, rather
than a narrow conception of the means of production. For Bahro
the concept of a cultural revolution addresses the question of
the kind of changes required in the present to begin to achieve
general human emancipation. It constitutes a shift away from
a common tendency within socialist thought to regard socialism
as a more productive and rational form of capitalism - a tendency
which is associated with the strategy of economic competition
with capitalism and with the deferment of the creation of communism until a future epoch when the general level of economic
production will be of a sufficient magnitude. If the creation of
communism awaits the maturation of the forces of production its
moment may never come. Thus Bahro has argued for a shift of
priorities away from those associated with 'the old socialists and
communists' and scientific Marxists.

Analysis of the societies of actually existing socialism has
revealed that obstacles to human self-realisation are not confined merely to the effect of a capitalist class structure; rather
they are also a consequence of relations of domination which
may endure beyond capitalism. In particular the unquestioned
adoption of scientific and technological rationality and the
associated equation of growth with progress has in Bahro's
view constituted a 'stabilizing agency for the present relations
of domination' (ibid., p. 265). Given this, Bahro has commented
that it is no longer appropriate to refer to the hegemony of the
proletariat; what is required is a new social revolution, nothing
less than the creation of a consensus among all the progressive
social forces. However, an appropriate political forum for the
construction of an ideological consensus and an organisational
framework for cultural revolution is lacking. The existing political organisation, the party, has become synonymous with the
bureaucratic machine and is therefore unable to provide a basis
for opposition to existing relations of domination. Thus Bahro
has concluded that a new organisation is required to replace
the bankrupt bureaucratic party - a new forum, the League
of Communists, which should seek to engender communism as a
mass movement oriented to the achievement of general emancipation. Such a forum must avoid the re-creation of a bureaucratic form of organisation and the associated reconstitution of
subalternity. It must nurture emancipatory interests and seek
to create a consensus or broad alliance of all progressive
social forces. However, attractive and desirable as Bahro's
recommendations may seem, they remain as yet unrealised, and
in the light of the events of 1968 in Czechoslovakia and 1981-2
in Poland they seem remote and barely feasible.

THEORY AND PRACTICE

The respective dimensions of the theoretical and political crisis
of Marxism ultimately converge in the focal issue of the relationship between theory and practice. This relationship has assumed
a special significance for Marxists and has been derived from
the embryonic formulation of a philosophy of practice in the
'Theses on Feuerbach', particularly the eleventh thesis, which
affirms the importance of changing rather than merely interpret-
ing the world.

There have been several versions of the theory-practice
relationship within the history of Marxism, but generally the
unity of theory and practice has been conceptualised as an
ideal to be realised in the future. The terms in which the relationship has been conceptualised may have varied from a relation
between 'Marxist theory' and 'proletarian practice' to one between theoretical practice and political practice; however, a
consistent underlying feature of each of the respective formulations has been the problematic status of the relationship. Indeed,
as Anderson has remarked, even though Marx and Engels may
have achieved moments of coincidence between theory and practice, in their work also there was 'never an unbroken or
immediate identity.... The relationship ... was thus always
uneven and mediate' (1976, p. 3).

Contemporary Marxism has operated with two basic formulations of the theory-practice relationship. The most common
formulation has been that of the possibility of an intimate, dialectical relationship between theory and practice, of the possibility of realising theory in practice. Here we are on quite
familiar ground, but a ground not specific to Marxism alone
(cf. Gramsci, 1976, pp. 364-5). The validity and rationality
of theory and the necessity and rationality of practice are
simultaneously demonstrated through the identification of a
unity of theory and practice. For Marxism the problem has been
that the conception of an apparent or possible unity has been
shattered by evidence of the problems of actually existing
socialism, in particular the continuation, perhaps even the
exacerbation, of relations of domination, and by the decline or
absence of revolutionary working-class movements in the West.
In consequence analysis has addressed the question of the
preconditions for the reunification of theory and practice, the
construction of a 'new unity of socialist theory and working
class practice' (Anderson, 1976, p. 104).

However, from the very beginning there has been a problem.
In so far as Marxist theory has conventionally been the specialist
activity of intellectuals of bourgeois origin, there has inevitably
been an imbalance within the theory-practice relationship: it
has always been a matter of the theoretical representation of
the interests of the working class being in the hands of an
intellectual-party vanguard. Hence the argument that the mistakes and pitfalls associated with the classical and Western

Marxist traditions may only be resolved by the rise of a mass
revolutionary movement which has successfully generated its
own organic intellectuals (cf. Gramsci, 1976, pp. 5-23). If such
a development is possible, it will denote a new phase in the
history of Marxism: it will constitute a break not only with the
tradition of Western Marxism but also with the classical tradition, for in both cases Marxist theory has been the product of
'traditional' or bourgeois intellectuals. In the classical tradition
there may have been moments of coincidence between socialist
theory and political practice, but these were largely confined
to the formal membership of traditional Marxist intellectuals in
political movements, the adoption of elements of their analyses
in the development of strategies for engineering social changes
and reforms, and the analysis of the effects or outcomes of
specific political struggles as appropriate grounds for the revi-
sion of theoretical concepts and analysis. In Western Marxism
theoretical and philosophical analyses have become increasingly
divorced from political practice. However, in both traditions
intellectuals have performed a leading role in the formulation
of political analysis and strategy; they have constituted, in the
sense that Lenin regarded as necessary, a vanguard force.

One response to the disunity of theory and practice and the
continuing absence of any mass revolutionary movement in the
advanced industrial societies has been to regard the events of
1968 and the reappearance of a world-wide capitalist recession
as signifying that there may be a genuine 'chance of a revolutionary circuit reopening between Marxist theory and mass
practice, looped through real struggles of the industrial working class' (Anderson, 1976, p. 96). Notable in this position is
a familiar emphasis upon the struggles of the industrial working class and the presence of a conception of politics that
remains deeply rooted in the economy. Furthermore, although
Anderson has admitted that the specific form of future theory
cannot be anticipated, and that we should not presume a mere
repetition of classical Marxist models, his conclusion constitutes
a promotion of the legacy of Trotsky and leaves the final word
to Lenin. Thus we are returned to the classical tradition, to
their 'solution', and to the familiar prescription that 'correct
theory' may only be acquired by way of a close connection with
the practical activity of a truly revolutionary proletariat. We
have, of course, come full circle, to a restatement of the central
article of faith, namely of the possibility of a unity of theory
and practice. The practical problems associated with the realisation of a unity are thus left in abeyance.

The second formulation of the theory-practice relationship
within Marxism has made a virtue of necessity by conceptualising the gap or distance between theory and practice as an
inevitability. One version of this position may be found in
Anderson's self-critical reflections on the work I have referred
to above. Basically the position adopted is that the 'tenet of
the unity of theory and practice' has been assumed rather than

investigated and that as soon as it has been subjected to critical analysis it has become apparent that there 'will always remain an inherent scissiparity between knowledge and action, theory and practice, for any possible science of history' (1976, p. 110). However, the observation made by Anderson, and the comparable position outlined by Poulantzas (1978, p. 22), namely that the orthodox formula and assumed universality of the unity of theory and practice is now inadmissible, does not resolve the matter, for it leaves unanswered the question of the relationship between the discourse of Marxism, political practice and its effect. I will return to this issue in my discussion of the work of Foucault.

3   REACTION, REVISION AND CRITICISM

At the heart of the contemporary crisis of Marxism is the question of the relationship between Marxist discourse and socialist political practice. The tendency has been for this question to be reformulated in terms of an examination of the relationship between Marxist theory and analysis and the reality of the societies of actually existing socialism. There have been a series of quite different responses to the question of the relationship between Marxist discourse, political practice and its effects. These have ranged from attempts by dissident intellectuals in Eastern Europe to disentangle and then to dissociate an 'authentic' Marxism from the reality of life within the societies of actually existing socialism, to the assertions of the 'new philosophers' that Marx is dead and that the socialism made in his name is equivalent to a form of totalitarianism (cf. Lévy, 1979; Glucksmann, 1980). Between these two diametrically opposed positions there are a variety of 'Eurocommunist' reformulations of Marxist theory and political strategy, derived in large part from the work of Gramsci, and in addition Foucault's construction of a new form of critical analysis.

Although all these responses to Marxism may be differentiated from one another on several counts, they do share a common reference, namely a critical orientation to the societies of actually existing socialism. In each case these societies have been conceptualised as fundamentally limited and limiting, as no longer representing a desirable model for social development. However, as we shall see, there are substantial differences between the respective positions over the question of the extent to which Marxist theory and analysis may be charged with a degree of responsibility for the deficiencies or pathologies associated with the societies of actually existing socialism.

In this chapter I will briefly consider particular responses to the question of the relationship between Marxist theory and analysis and the reality of the socialist societies emanating from the following sources:

   (i) Soviet and Eastern European dissidents
  (ii) Eurocommunism
 (iii) The 'new philosophers'

All too frequently criticism of Marxism or of the societies of actually existing socialism has been interpreted as a de facto endorsement of the assumed antithesis, namely a reactionary, conservative, politics of the Right, or a celebration of the virtues of the capitalist system. Because Marxism has constituted the principal source of a vocabulary through which to articulate opposition to the prevailing social order, fundamental criticism of its central tenets, conceptions, and effects has been regarded as synonymous with the neutralisation of critique, or worse, with the affirmation and development of a vocabulary which gives hostage to the Right. The possibility of criticism having such an effect has not only produced various forms of self-censorship but, within Eastern Europe and the Soviet Union, it has constituted the basis on which the policing and repression of criticism has been legitimised.

The polarisation of political thought into shades of Left and Right has provided no place for anything other than 'fraternal' criticism. One is either a 'friend' or an 'enemy', and whichever it is one's credentials must be in order - of such is the poverty of our existing political culture composed.

DISSENT IN EASTERN EUROPE AND THE SOVIET UNION

The existence of various forms of opposition, resistance and dissent within the societies of actually existing socialism - what we might term the 'Soviet-type societies' (cf. Wildt, 1979) - is indisputable, as indeed is the absurdity of the official attribution of all such forms of conflict to the activities of a minority of 'bourgeois', and by implication misguided, intellectuals, the 'class enemy', or the hidden hand of the CIA and American imperialism. We might note the similarity between the strategical response of the state in the societies of Eastern Europe to dissent and protest and the tendency in the West for 'extra-parliamentary' forms of opposition to be accounted for in terms of the destabilising activities of 'activists', 'Trotskyists' or communists financed by Moscow. In both instances fundamental forms of opposition and protest have been regarded as signifying the sinister presence of alien political interests seeking to foment a disruption of the utilitarian, social equilibrium synonymous with the existing social and economic order.

Within Eastern Europe and the Soviet Union there have been a series of expressions of opposition to particular features of the socialist system which have received broad public support. For example, in 1953 in the German Democratic Republic a section of the working class, the 'social foundation', protested against the communist government and its policies; in 1956, 1970, 1976 and again in 1980/1 in Poland there were significant protests and forms of opposition against the state; in 1956 in Hungary and in 1968 in Czechoslovakia popular reforms of the socialist system were achieved and subsequently withdrawn by military intervention which sought to restore the status quo despite fierce public opposition; in the Soviet Union since 1965, beginning with the arrest and trial of Siniavski and Daniel, there have been a series of public protests against the trials of dissidents, principally intellectuals (cf. Feldbrugge, 1975), and in addition a whole series of less celebrated 'workers' protests and strikes (cf. Holubenko, 1975; Haynes and Semyonova, 1979). Generally the expression of opposition has been focused either on the economic contradictions and problems of the socialist system, at its simplest, on the apparent inability of the system to deliver the goods, or, alternatively, on the repressive effect of the centralisation of political power, most notably the infringement of fundamental human rights.

Given the single-party representational structure embodied in the form of the state in Eastern Europe, its associated hypersensitivity to criticism, and the attendant facility with which the articulation of opposition has been silenced by charging authors with infringement of specific articles of the criminal law, in particular those concerning anti-state agitation and propaganda and defamation of the state through the circulation of 'false' documents (cf. Amnesty International, 1975), it is not surprising to find that critical analyses have largely been confined to 'samizdat'. 'Samizdat', a term derived from 'samsebiaizdat', which literally means 'publishing house for oneself', refers to the series of illegal or underground networks for the production and circulation of documents and analyses which would otherwise be withheld from circulation or publication. A selection of this work has been published in the West and it is largely from such sources that I will be drawing my observations.

However, before proceeding to a discussion of the forms of oppositional thought which have emerged in the 'Soviet-type societies', in which I will concentrate upon the Soviet Union, a few brief qualifications are in order. To begin with, the very illegality of the expression of dissent and opposition, whether in the form of texts or actions, has meant that opposition groups have, at best, been loosely organised. Indeed, their very survival has depended upon it. In consequence the identity of opposition groupings has been somewhat ambiguous and their respective analyses have tended to lack clarity. Where a degree of clarification has emerged it has been attributable to the statements of individuals who have proclaimed themselves to be 'true' Marxists, 'loyal' Leninists, democrats, liberals or whatever. Therefore, any classification we choose to employ is liable to lack precision. Nevertheless, qualifications aside, a simple and helpful distinction may be drawn between critical analyses of the experience of living in a socialist society which simultaneously seek to preserve the possibility of 'true' communism or Marxism, or to retain a loyalty to Leninism, and those critical analyses which are explicitly non-Marxist, perhaps anti-Leninist, pro-Western and/or liberal. Through such categories we may differentiate between the views of the likes of Medvedev and Solzhenitsyn, or Grigorenko and Sakharov.

Within the Soviet Union we may differentiate between the following relatively distinct oppositional groupings (cf. Feldbrugge, 1975):

(i) Marxist-Leninists
(ii) socialists
(iii) democrats
(iv) nationalists

The analysis of the Marxist-Leninist opposition has taken the
following general form. The major defects of the Soviet system
have been identified as a product of a departure from genuinely
Leninist policies. Thus the problems evident in the Soviet Union
and elsewhere in Eastern Europe have been identified as originating
with the advent of Stalin and the construction of a monolithic bureaucracy, which reduced the concept of the dictatorship of the proletariat to the exercise of power through a
centralised state apparatus by a privileged minority. The
remedy proposed, at its simplest, seems to require a return to
Lenin and a creative development of his ideas.

However, the explanation of the problems manifested by the
Soviet-type societies in terms of the role of Stalin and an
associated tendency towards bureaucratic centralism, deemed
necessary for rapid industrialisation and collectivisation after
the revolution, has left several controversial issues unresolved.
Contemporary Soviet society, along with the other Eastern
European states, has continued to be dominated by a relatively
small and privileged group of people whose rule has been
guaranteed through the pervasiveness of the system of surveillance deployed throughout the society by the bureaucratic
apparatus. Throughout the Soviet-type societies there has been
a general lack of personal freedom, of civil and human rights,
and an absence of any satisfactory mechanism through which
the will of the people might be expressed. In addition to political inequalities arising from the absence of democratic procedures, social and economic inequalities have continued to be a
consistent feature of the Soviet-type societies. All these features are inconsistent with expectations which have been
derived from the texts of classical Marxism, for example that
socialism would ensure the broadest possible form of democracy,
hasten the dismantling of the bureaucratic state apparatus,
and provide the appropriate means for a transition to greater
social equality.

The Marxist-Leninist opposition has had to respond to each
of the objections advanced by other, less sympathetic opponents
of the Soviet-type societies. Ultimately its position has required
the generation of a fine distinction between the failures and
limitations of the existing social and economic order which has
been subjected to criticism and the, as yet, unrealised possibilities of Marxism. The criticisms of the current social and
economic order in Eastern Europe advanced by the Marxist-
Leninist opposition have been grounded in the resurrected
goals of the October Revolution and the Leninist vision. However, the shadow of Stalin has not been dispelled, for the other
opposition groups have remained unconvinced that Lenin bore

no responsibility for the bureaucratisation of Soviet society, that the priority accorded to the party over the proletariat, and to the state bureacracy over the trade unions, did not provide the essential preconditions for Stalinism.

The socialist opposition has shared a degree of common ground with the Marxist-Leninist opposition, in particular over the questions of the poor performance of the Soviet economy and the continued existence of a highly privileged bureaucratic elite. However, the socialists have rejected the need to defend Marxism-Leninism and, in addition, have argued that the October Revolution merely ushered in a form of bureaucratic state capitalism, rather than socialism. In their criticisms of the centralisation of power in the bureaucratic state apparatus they have argued that the bureaucratic elite constitutes a class and that there has existed a fundamental antagonism between this group and the intelligentsia. Their indictment of the bureaucratic elite, namely that it has curtailed the freedom necessary for the intelligentsia adequately to perform its critical function in an advanced industrial society, is indicative of the direction in which they would like the Soviet-type societies to develop, namely towards a recognition of the potentially progressive role of the intelligentsia. Two equally important additional and associated demands advanced by the socialists are that government of the people should be exercised through a democratically elected body, and that state ownership of the means of production, the principal source of the monopolistic power of the bureaucracy, should be abolished. Such demands have driven a firm wedge between the Marxist-Leninist and socialist opposition movements.

The democratic opposition has constituted the largest of the dissident groups. The most distinctive features of their analysis have been the preoccupation with human and civil rights and the presence of a positive disposition towards Western-democratic political forms. Although they have also shared the criticisms of the Soviet system developed by the Marxist-Leninist and socialist opposition groups, their position has ultimately been significantly differentiated by their conception of the October Revolution as an economically and politically regressive event. In their view the revolution has been responsible for the destruction of many positive social values; it has precipitated a further erosion of public freedom and has slowed down the growth of public welfare. It is not surprising, therefore, to find that the democratic opposition has concluded that capitalism constitutes the system most conducive to the promotion of general economic welfare and to the achievement of a decent standard of living, and further that such a system seems to provide the most suitable environment for the development and preservation of human rights. Finally, at the basis of the democratic movement's programme has been the demand for a democratisation of the political system, for an installation of the institutions of Western parliamentary democracy.

However, just as the Marxist-Leninist opposition has been
vulnerable to the criticism that it has failed to account satisfactorily for the departure of the Soviet-type societies from the
Leninist road to socialism, so the democratic opposition has been
equally vulnerable to the criticism that its analysis has revealed
a hasty embrace of Western capitalism and a concomitant neglect
of any examination of the possibility of an alternative or genuine
form of socialism.

The final category of opposition is that represented by the
various nationalist groups, what we might term the representa-
tives of the non-Russian communities. The principal focus of
their opposition has been the process of 'Russification' and the
associated infringements of the rights of the various minority
nationalities (e.g. Ukranians, Lithuanians, Estonians, Jews,
Crimean Tartars, Volga Germans). Essentially the nationalist
groups have been demanding autonomy from Moscow, more freedom and the scope for self-determination. In some cases national-
istic demands have been associated with unfulfilled socialist
aspirations. We need to remember, however, that considerable
differences have remained between the various nationalist
opposition groups over the question of the desirability of socialism and the value of Marxism-Leninism. Nevertheless, it is once
again evident that there has been a high degree of concordance
with the other opposition groups over general criticisms of the
repression of human rights and political freedoms by the bureaucratic state apparatus.

I have noted that the various opposition groups have shared
particular criticisms of Soviet society, although the extent of
their criticisms, the degree to which problems have been attributed to socialism or to Marxism-Leninism, and their subsequent
proposals for reforms and changes, have varied considerably.
In each case there has been a clearly articulated opposition to
the infringement of human rights, the absence of political freedoms, and the employment of the criminal law, often in a manner
which has violated the constitution, to repress opposition and
peaceful protest.

In the West the violations of basic human rights associated
with the Soviet-type societies have come to be regarded as
incontrovertible signs of a moral decadence and decay. They
have also been accepted in some quarters as evidence of the
necessarily inhumane and undesirable nature of socialism and
of the deleterious consequences of the attempted implementation
of Marxism. This issue has become known as the 'Gulag question'
and its most explicit formulation has appeared in the work of
Solzhenitsyn.

'THE GULAG ARCHIPELAGO'

Solzhenitsyn has, in many respects, constituted a reactionary
figure. Since his involuntary exile in the West he has displayed

an alarming political innocence or naivety in his choice of asso-
ciates and sponsors. However, his work - in particular, that on
the network of prison camps in the Soviet Union, 'The Gulag
Archipelago' - has retained its stature, not merely because it
remains a major literary achievement but in addition because it
stirred 'the conscience of a society in whose name terrible crimes
have been perpetrated' (Deutscher, 1976, p. 107).

Although Solzhenitsyn's work constitutes an 'artistic investigation' rather than a scientific analysis of historical events, it
has been accepted that the main facts, notably the details of
those imprisoned and their treatment, are correct (cf. Medvedev,
1974a). 'The Gulag Archipelago' contains several stories, tales
of arrest, interrogation, trial, sentence and incarceration, the
material for which has been drawn from Solzhenitsyn's own
experiences, from interviews with a great many former prisoners
and from documentary material, including official publications.
Each account conveys a sense of the terror and injustice to
which successive sections of the community have been subjected.

For Solzhenitsyn the process of institutionalised terror is
virtually synonymous with the aftermath of the October Revolution, for its origin may be traced right back to Lenin. For
example, at the end of 1917 Lenin expressed the view that it was
necessary to establish strict revolutionary order: it was important to suppress anarchy and counter-revolution wherever it
was identified. In particular Lenin urged that it was necessary
to develop 'practical forms and methods of accounting and con-
trolling' in order 'to *clean* the land of Russia of all vermin'
(1964, p. 414). Now this may appear to be nothing more than a
relatively harmless metaphorical statement: however, as Solzhenitsyn has noted, Lenin had in mind not only all class enemies,
but also indolent workers and 'slovenly and hysterical intellectuals'. Furthermore, the process of purging extended from
arrest and imprisonment, and punishment at forced labour, down
to the final solution of the shooting of 'parasites'.

Solzhenitsyn has indicated that the elasticity and ambiguity of
the terms employed to identify the sections of the community
from which opposition and resistance might arise lent itself to
exploitation in the form of an expansion of the groups and
organisations subjected to investigation and prosecution. All
manner of people were classified as the source of potential dis-
order and opposition. For example, Solzhenitsyn has suggested
that people in the cooperative movement, in teaching, on the
parish councils, on the railways and in the trade unions were
often identified as hostile to the working class, not to mention
the 'many kinds of cursed intellectuals there were ... who are
always a hindrance to a well-ordered strict regime' (Solzhenitsyn,
1980, p. 28).

The purging of such a vast number of people would have been
virtually impossible if normal legal processes and judicial procedures had been followed; certainly it would have taken an
inordinate amount of time. In order to cope with the vast number

of suspects a new form of procedure was adopted, combining 'investigation, arrest, interrogation, prosecution, trial, and execution of the *verdict*' (ibid., p. 28) in the hands of the Cheka. Therefore, in the period before the establishment of a criminal code, or of a new system of criminal law, the Cheka was able to institutionalise specific operational procedures and to employ all the relevant techniques and disciplines at its disposal for the 'processing' of suspects with the utmost 'efficiency'.

Solzhenitsyn has documented a whole series of purges, what he terms 'waves', which swept Socialist Revolutionaries, Mensheviks, Anarchists, and Popular Socialists into the camps along with Russians returning from abroad, students guilty of criticising the system, peasants who had contested the state's requisitioning of food – anyone, indeed, whose political credentials were in doubt. Now, although the main body of Solzhenitsyn's work has been focused on the Gulag under Stalin, it is clear that the origin of the associated institutions and practices has not been attributed solely to that particular 'cult of personality', even though some of the more extreme excesses might have been. For Solzhenitsyn the practice of institutionalised terror not only existed prior to Stalin but, in addition, survived him, and Khrushchev's cosmetic liberalisations. Indeed, although Stalin may have been described as the supreme architect of the Gulag Archipelago, the existence of the camps has been depicted as inextricably linked to the existing political system and, by implication therefore, to socialism. As Solzhenitsyn has cryptically commented:

> Rulers change, the Archipelago remains. It remains because *that particular* political regime could not survive without it. If it disbanded the Archipelago, it would cease to exist itself. (1978, p. 494)

Thus the Gulag has become, for Solzhenitsyn, an inevitable consequence of the October Revolution and its aftermath, namely the construction of a socialist society.

Reaction to Solzhenitsyn's powerful prose has been mixed, ranging from the uncritical response of the 'new philosophers', for whom Solzhenitsyn's work has been not so much revelatory as instructive on 'how to resist the *Gulag* [and] how to perceive it from inside the system' (cf. 'Time', 1977, p. 9), to the measured criticisms of Medvedev (1974a) and Mandel (1974), to which I will now turn. Both Medvedev and Mandel seem to have accepted the validity of many of Solzhenitsyn's observations on the Stalinist repression, although Mandel has categorically rejected the implication that at root Lenin (and behind him Marx and Engels) could in any way have been responsible for the excesses of Stalin.

Mandel's position constitutes a not unfamiliar defence of the October Revolution, of Marxism-Leninism, and of the possibility of socialism. Solzhenitsyn's intervention is, at best, ranked

alongside the prior contribution of Trotsky in 'The Revolution
Betrayed' and in 'The Crimes of Stalin'. However, Mandel has
offered a compensatory qualification, namely that even though
'The Gulag Archipelago' may contain nothing new, it does contain 'unforgettable sketches' of specific individuals. The merits
of the text have therefore been equated with its literary qualities rather than with its historical or political analyses. Indeed,
the latter dimensions have been identified by Mandel as the
source of the limitations of the text. Briefly, he has argued that
there are two major deficiencies in Solzhenitsyn's work: a
heavily one-sided preoccupation with 'the red terror', and a concomitant silence on 'the white terror' which precipitated the
Bolsheviks' response (e.g. the armed attacks on Bolshevik
leaders; the invasion of Soviet territory by foreign armies),
and in addition a general inability to explain events, other than
in terms of an invoked 'ideological fanaticism', for which, Mandel
has suggested, we should read revolutionary Marxism, which
Solzhenitsyn has condemned.

Mandel's line is that Lenin and Trotsky cannot reasonably be
held responsible for the excesses of Stalin. Indeed, he has
argued that

under Lenin and Trotsky, there were no confessions extrac-
ted under torture, that the accused were able to defend
themselves freely - and not without a chance of success -
that these trials were hardly witch-hunt trials, but rather
revolutionary ones, doubtlessly sometimes based on circum-
stantial and insufficient evidence, as is always the case in a
revolutionary period, but a thousand miles removed from the
caricatures of justice staged by Stalin. (1974, p. 54)

In this way Mandel has sought to refute the challenge mounted
by Solzhenitsyn to the legitimacy and desirability of the October
revolution, to distance this event and its immediate history
from the 'Stalinist and post-Stalinist terror', and thereby to
absolve Marxism-Leninism from responsibility for the Gulag.
Of course, Mandel has accepted that the Soviet regime has been
guilty of errors; however, these have been described as the
almost inevitable consequence of the problems confronting
leaders who had the formidable honour of being the first in
history to construct a state in the service of the workers and
of the exploited' (ibid., p. 55). With hindsight it is relatively
easy to agree with the view that the dangers of counter-
revolution were indeed grossly overestimated, that administra-
tive repression would almost certainly produce demoralisation
amongst the proletariat, and that the institutionalisation of one-
party rule would ultimately lead to a dictatorship of the bureaucracy. However, Mandel has argued, at the time the Bolsheviks
could not know the consequences of their policies, or the dread-
fully problematic legacy they would bequeath to the socialist
movement. When balancing accounts we are asked to try to

understand the context in which the Bolsheviks found themselves, to reflect upon the reality of Bolshevik justice, bearing
in mind the excesses which might have followed from a victorious
'white terror'.

Mandel has concluded his discussion of 'The Gulag Archipelago'
with a defence of Marxism and an ironic comment on the consequences of Solzhenitsyn's work. He has suggested that there is
a 'dialectical interplay between Solzhenitsyn and the Soviet
bureaucracy', by which he means that Solzhenitsyn's work has
served to provide the Kremlin with clear proof that the opposition in the USSR is indeed counter-revolutionary, anti-Marxist,
and possessed of an anti-socialist ideology. Unwittingly, therefore, Solzhenitsyn's work has served to legitimate the repression of opposition and the censorship of criticism. For Mandel
the way forward needs must involve support for the movement
for democratic rights in the USSR for the right to speak, write,
and participate in criticism of the regime. Thus, even though
he rejects Solzhenitsyn's analysis, its prescribed enlightened
authoritarianism, espousal of religion and nationalism, and
concomitant rejection of Marxism, he has emphasised the importance of defending the right to 'speak, discuss, publish and
organize' of which Solzhenitsyn, Grigorenko, and generations
of other dissidents have been deprived.

Medvedev's (1974a) critical appraisal of Solzhenitsyn's work
may be differentiated from Mandel's reaction in at least two
important respects. First, it has emanated from within the heart
of the dissident movement in the Soviet Union, and second it
reveals a greater willingness to consider the possibility of
Lenin's responsibility for the provision of at least some of the
preconditions of Stalinism. Medvedev's appraisal opens with a
comment on the transparently fraudulent character of the
regime's critical response to Solzhenitsyn's work, namely that
his facts were 'incorrect' ('Pravda'), or by way of a contrast,
that the book 'contained nothing new' ('Literaturnaya Gazeta').
Medvedev has argued not only that he personally learnt much
from Solzhenitsyn's work, but that there is a general ignorance
over the facts presented in 'The Gulag Archipelago'.

The other line of criticism to which Solzhenitsyn's work has
frequently been subjected is that it neglects other evils, namely
those of Nazism and of Russian Tsarism. This is a bit like criticising the author for not writing on another topic, although,
as Medvedev has commented, even on that score Solzhenitsyn
is beyond criticism, for he makes several references to the suf-
fering of Russian prisoners under the Nazis. To underline his
defence of Solzhenitsyn Medvedev has added that, in any event,
Stalin not only unleashed mass repressions long before Hitler
achieved power, but did so on a scale that admits of no comparison with the less significant Tsarist period (cf. 1974a, p. 29).

Where Medvedev has parted company from Solzhenitsyn is
over the question of the specific role of Stalin, or to be more
precise, over the issue of the relationship of Stalin and Stalinism

to the October Revolution and to Lenin. Medvedev has quite
correctly observed that, although Solzhenitsyn's work is principally about the Stalinist terror, the personal role of Stalin has
been relegated to the periphery. Stalin has been portrayed as
merely a 'blind and perfunctory executive agent' (Solzhenitsyn,
1980, p. 68, n. 35), following in the much larger footsteps of
Lenin. This brings us to the crux of the matter, to the critical
significance of Solzhenitsyn's work for contemporary political
strategy, namely its identification of Lenin and the founders
of scientific socialism as bearing responsibility for the deforma-
tions of the Soviet system, and for the Gulag in particular.

Medvedev has expressed criticism of Solzhenitsyn's repudia-
tion of Marxism-Leninism because of its responsibility for the
defects evident in the Soviet Union. His criticism has taken
two forms. On the one hand he has argued that 'true' Marxism-
Leninism, 'the point of departure for the development of scientific socialism and scientific communism' (cf. 1974b, p. 70), is,
like every other science, at times imprecise and mistaken, but
that it cannot be charged with all the limitations and defects of
the Soviet Union. Indeed, the implication of his comments is
that it was the Stalinist departure from Marxism-Leninism which
produced the system of which Solzhenitsyn has quite rightly
been critical. Medvedev has therefore attempted to defend
Marxism-Leninism's credentials, its scientificity, from Solzhenitsyn's indictment that it has assumed the status of a dogma. The
second dimension of Medvedev's criticism of Solzhenitsyn's work
follows logically from the above and concerns the rupture (or
link) between Lenin and Stalin.

Whereas Solzhenitsyn has argued that Lenin forced Russia
through a revolution for which it was unready, employed
unjustifiable methods against political opponents, and thereby
prepared the foundations for Stalinism, Medvedev has responded
by arguing that

> within the framework of the relations between Party, State,
> and society created in Russia under Lenin, Stalin effected
> sharp turns and fundamental reversals, merely preserving
> the outward shell of so-called Leninist norms and the official
> vocabulary of Marxism-Leninism. (1974a, p. 30)

Further, although Medvedev has acknowledged that Lenin and
his government committed a great many errors, he has expressed the view that it is not possible to establish either that the
revolution was premature, or that the excesses of Stalin might
be attributable to mistakes committed by Lenin.

Nevertheless, whilst attempting to distance 'true' Marxism-
Leninism from the excesses of Stalinism, and complaining of the
misspent opportunities created by the October Revolution for
the construction of a genuinely socialist and democratic society,
Medvedev has referred to the very kind of abuse of power which
has precipitated the 'Gulag question' and an extension of the

chain of responsibility back to Lenin, and ultimately to Marx
and Engels. Specifically, he has commented that

> It is unfortunately true that in the early years of the Revo-
> lution, Lenin too used the verb 'shoot' much more often than
> existing circumstances demanded... would anyone today
> approve, for example, of the following order sent in August
> 1918 by Lenin ... 'No efforts to be spared; mass terror to
> be introduced, *hundreds* of prostitutes who have intoxicated
> our soldiers, and former officers, etc., to be shot and
> deported'. (Ibid., p. 32)

Although Medvedev has recognised that many acts of mass
violence such as this were harmful and unnecessary, he remains
convinced that the 'overall balance sheet of Lenin's activity was
positive'. The grounds for this judgment seem, however, to lie
less with the facts, with evidence, or proof, than with a desire
to preserve the possibility of a restoration of a 'true' Marxism-
Leninism and a reconstruction of the road to a genuinely democratic and socialist society.

EUROCOMMUNIST ALTERNATIVES

The expression of opposition and criticism in the Soviet Union
and in Eastern Europe, exemplified by the activities of the
various dissident movements and the writings of prominent
individuals such as Solzhenitsyn, Sakharov, Medvedev, and
Bahro, has contributed, along with the impact of such events
as the Prague Spring in 1968, to the emergence of relatively
independent conceptions of socialism and socialist strategy in
Western Europe. The persistence and scale of repression in the
societies of actually existing socialism, whether it has taken
the form of the incarceration by a specific state of the communist Left in camps and prisons and the voluntary or involuntary exile of the reactionary Right (cf. Deutscher, 1976), or
the more 'external' form of an orchestrated invasion of a
fraternal state in order to 'save' socialism from allegedly reactionary forces, has created the context in which Western European communist parties have found it necessary to relinquish
their endorsement of barbarous policies and to confront the
uncomfortable realisation that there is no longer any model for
socialism. Instead of continuing to remain in the shadow of their
more 'progressive' Eastern European peers, Western European
communist parties have proceeded to advance fundamental
criticisms of actually existing socialism and of the central and
guiding tenets of Marxist theory (cf. Valenta, 1980). Their
conclusions seem to have been that the possibility of political
advancement depends upon a willingness to explore not only the
question of a democratic road to socialism, but the very idea of
socialism itself as a possible and desirable form of society.

The concept of 'Eurocommunism' is both ambiguous and controversial, for it suggests that there may be a new 'European'
form of communism and, furthermore, that the respective European communist parties may share a common policy, conception
of politics, and strategy. In practice the term has excluded
the Eastern European communist parties and has referred exclu-
sively to the various communist parties in Western capitalist
societies which have sought to adapt their respective conceptions of socialism and communism, and strategies of transition,
to the realities of life within advanced capitalism, and in the
process have found it necessary to diverge from the form of
socialism associated with the Soviet Union and Eastern Europe.
The term may apply not only to the Communist Party of Italy
(PCI) and the Communist Party of Spain (PCE), but also to the
communist parties of Great Britain and Sweden, as well as to
those of Japan and Australia (cf. Claudin, 1978; della Torre
et al., 1979). However, although there has been common ground
between these parties, there have also been not inconsiderable
differences of analysis and policy.

Behind all the differences between the PCI, the PCE, and the
other 'Eurocommunist' parties, there has remained a common
rejection and criticism of Soviet-style communism and a concomitant emphasis upon the fundamental significance of democratic procedures and practices as the foundation for the con- -
struction of a new socialist society, a society which, as Berlinguer has proposed, 'will guarantee all freedoms – personal and
collective, civil and religious – the non-ideological character of
the state, the possibility for different parties to exist side by
side, and pluralism in society, culture and ideals' (quoted in
Levi, 1979, p. 15). Paradoxically, a conception of the necessary
interdependence of socialism with freedom and democracy has
coexisted with a tendency in the Eurocommunist parties to continue to regard the Eastern European and Soviet regimes as
socialist, albeit in a minimal sense, and this even though freedom and democracy under these regimes have been, if not
entirely absent, certainly highly restricted. Undoubtedly this
contradiction has constituted a legacy of the historical relationship of the Eurocommunist parties to the October Revolution and
its aftermath. There still remains the last vestige of a hope that
the Eastern European and Soviet regimes are moving, albeit
slowly, along the road to socialism. How long the Eurocommunist
parties will be able to retain their faith in the societies of
actually existing socialism, whilst increasingly emphasising the
importance of a democratic road to socialism, is a matter of conjecture. Currently it would seem that the Eurocommunist parties
have more in common with the various dissident movements in
Eastern Europe than with the ruling bureaucratic party apparatuses which have claimed guardianship of socialism.

Within the history of Marxism the concept of democracy seems
to have evaded clarification. Although Marx and Engels asserted
in the 'Manifesto of the Communist Party' that the decisive

'first step in the revolution by the working class is to raise the
proletariat to the position of ruling class, to win the battle of
democracy' (1973, p. 86), they neglected to articulate their
conception of democracy. Likewise Lenin made reference to the
role of democracy in the anti-capitalist struggle and to the
impossibility of socialism without democracy, and similarly failed
to clarify his conception of democracy. The difficulty has been
that of not knowing what remains of democracy and democratic
processes once the heavily criticised 'bourgeois' associations
and connotations of the concept have been stripped away.
Indeed, in so far as Lenin at times employed the concept of
democracy almost synonymously with bourgeois rule, and thereby sought to discredit democratic rights and freedom, the
impression has been conveyed that the process of criticism and
change would yield no residue (cf. Lenin, 1965, pp. 160-1,
465, 467).

Where a positive conception of democracy was advanced it
tended to take the form of 'proletarian democracy'. However,
the workers' councils in the Soviet Union which were intended
to be an embodiment of this particular form of democracy were
short-lived; they quickly succumbed to the centralised political
power of the party and state apparatus. The kindest interpretation which might be placed upon this development is that the
party should be seen to have been acting in the interests of
the revolution, combating counter-revolution and reaction, as
compensating for the relative backwardness and concomitant
vulnerability of the masses. However, it is but a short distance
from this familiar vanguardist position, where the party constitutes the source of authority on Marxist theory, or scientific
socialism, and the guardian of the historic interests of the
proletariat, to the point at which dictatorship is exercised,
through a monolithic bureaucratic structure, over the proletariat. As things stand, the system of government in the Soviet-
type societies represents the very antithesis of democracy, in
any form. Hence the decision reached by the various Eurocommunist parties that they would have to chart their own democratic road to socialism.

In adopting the principle of a democratic road to socialism
the Eurocommunist parties have drawn attention to a series of
complex and controversial theoretical and political issues. The
judgment that the limitations of the societies of actually existing
socialism are not features of a transitional stage has precipitated
a variety of critical appraisals, the most important of which have
concerned the question of the state in both Eastern and Western
Europe. For example, it has been argued that the identification
or fusion of strategic organisations (e.g. the union; the party)
with the state in the societies of actually existing socialism has
undermined and obstructed the development of new democratic
forms of representation and thereby has increased the risk of
further bureaucratisation and authoritarianism. This line of
reasoning has in turn precipitated a re-evaluation of representa-

tive institutions, one result of which has been that such institutions, general representative assemblies, are no longer conceptualised as purely or inevitably bourgeois forms, but rather
as an integral feature of modern societies (cf. Ingrao, 1979).
Therefore, in reflections on the appropriate form of socialist
strategy for Western Europe the Eurocommunist parties have
accorded a particular significance to the extension and development of democratic forms of representation and the preservation
of the associated virtues of institutional pluralism. Indeed, the
proposal (and possibility) of a new form of state allowing effective representation and participation in decision-making for the
whole of the people has been identified as an essential precondition for the emergence of the broad-based alliance of progressive political forces necessary for any advance towards socialism.
    Whilst for some theorists Eurocommunism has constituted a
closet 'social democracy', for others it has represented the
'acceptable' and, by implication, deceptive face of communism,
it being assumed that once in power a Eurocommunist party
would shed its democratic 'pretensions'. This latter position has
been exemplified by the work of the 'new philosophers', for
whom the attractiveness of Eurocommunism to critics of Marxism
has constituted something of a bizarre phenomenon.

THE 'NEW PHILOSOPHERS'

The term 'new philosophers' has been coined to describe the
work of a group of French intellectuals who have achieved a
degree of popularity and notoriety for their criticisms of Marxism and the socialist societies. Whether the ideas of this group
are either novel or the product of philosophical reasoning
warrants consideration; however, I do not intend to explore
that particular issue, nor the question of the appropriateness
of a collective identity for the disparate communications which
have issued from their ranks.
    The general response to the work of the 'new philosophers'
has been mixed. On the one hand, the mass media have eagerly
provided them with a public platform from which to mount their
rhetorical condemnation of Marxism and the Soviet-type societies, and in addition have contrived to construct a celebrity
status for some members of the group. On the other hand, their
very success in gaining access to the means of mass communication and in achieving an unusual degree of popularity, for
intellectuals, has made them vulnerable to the charge that their
ideas are shallow and lack any grounding in detailed inquiry.
Thus, they have been described as 'disc-jockeys' of ideas,
as intellectual playboys, as beneficiaries of the rise to prominence and power of the information apparatus, the mass media
(cf. Debray, 1981).
    The most significant and common element in the writings and
proclamations of the 'new philosophers' has been a general

condemnation of all forms of political ideology, and of Marxism in particular. Indeed, it is the existence of this particular common reference point in the work of specific individuals which led Lévy to make reference to the emergence of a 'new philosophy'. The position shared by the 'new philosophers' is that socialism has produced a powerful form of domination, what has been described as totalitarian regulation, rather than emancipation or liberation. In reaching this position the 'new philosophers' have accepted the Soviet-type societies as an embodiment of the reality and possible form of any socialism and in addition have charged Marxism with a degree of responsibility for the existence of this new form of domination.

A considerable part of the attractiveness or appeal of this position, in addition to its evident political value when placed within the conventional terms of reference of the 'Left-Right' dichotomy, has been derived from the fact that it has constituted an expression of disillusionment on the part of former 'Left' political activitists, individuals who have been accredited with a degree of involvement in radical politics and in the events of May '68. For example, Glucksmann, a key figure, was a member of the PCF, then a Maoist, and since 1968 has expressed increasing disillusionment with Marxism.

With the benefit of hindsight the 'new philosophers' have attempted to reappraise the events of May '68 and have concluded that they never were really comfortable within the disintegrating framework of Marxism, that the events which took place were not in accord with the Marxist dialectic of history, but rather were indicative of a fundamental shift in understanding and consciousness, of the emergence of a 'cultural fracture' (cf. Dews, 1980). Therefore, the forms of rebellion and resistance associated with the events of May '68 have been retrospectively conceptualised as signalling the twilight of Marxism, as revealing the limits and limitations of Marxist thought and politics. Adjacent to this conception of the inadequacies of Marxism is a criticism of the 'effects' or consequences of Marxist theory, of Marxism as the political science of domination.

Although the criticisms of the 'new philosophers' extend, in principle at least, beyond Marxism, their references seem to be confined solely to the Soviet-type societies in which Marxism has constituted the official ideology. In consequence, their denunciations of totalitarianism and their anti-statism appear to be synonymous with an anti-Marxism and a total rejection of the work of Marx. For the 'new philosophers' it would seem that socialism, especially in its Soviet form, represents the most highly developed form of totalitarianism, the ultimate realisation of technical rationality and social engineering.

At the highest level of generality the 'new philosophers' have argued that reason as such has become synonymous with domination, that reason is totalitarian, and that in so far as the emergence of the social and human sciences has been concomitant with the development of a modern instrumental form of reason, then these sciences have operated within, and have reinforced, existing relations of power. The distance from a general criticism of modern reason to an indictment of Marxism is but a short one for the 'new philosophers'. In their view, analysis of the form of life in the societies of actually existing socialism has not only shown that the state is the source of social and political oppression but, in addition, has revealed that such practices as the confinement of dissidents and the infringement of human rights are a natural and necessary feature of socialism. Furthermore, they have argued that Marxist theory may be held responsible, or alternatively considered culpable, in so far as it has generally failed to address or to account for such practices. Thus Marxism has been charged by the 'new philosophers', either with a direct responsibility for the existence of the particular form of socialism characteristic of Eastern Europe and the Soviet Union, or alternatively with having contributed to the circumstances in which the general reaction to the Gulag has been one of docility or non-resistance.

Both positions may be found in the work of Glucksmann. In his earlier work he argued that Marxism did indeed have to answer for the reality of the Gulag. His subsequent work has indicated a modification of this position, best exemplified by his statement:

> I reproach Marx with having traced a certain number of intellectual routes: the cult of the total and final Revolution, of the State that terrorizes for the good of the collectivity, and of social science that permits the masses to be guided in spite of themselves. These paths do not lead directly to the Gulag but to non-resistance to the Gulag. (1977, p. 97)

The concept of the Gulag, embraced by the 'new philosophers', has been derived from the work of Solzhenitsyn, 'the best historian of contemporary Russia' according to Glucksmann (ibid.). Now, although the reality of the Gulag is not in dispute, the concentration of the 'new philosophers' on this specific institution, and their concomitant neglect of other incidences of systematic internment of political opposition and of infringements of human rights, as documented by organisations such as Amnesty International, has raised doubts about their motives. One very plausible explanation which has been advanced to account for the general emphasis in the work of the 'new philosophers' on Marxism, socialism and the Gulag has referred to their respective biographies and to the possibility that their former 'Marxomania' may have been displaced by an equally exaggerated 'Marxophobia' (cf. Bobbio, 1979a). In this case they would join the ranks of earlier generations of former Marxists who have recanted and subsequently become the fiercest of critics.

In so far as the analyses of the 'new philosophers' have displayed a marked tendency towards superficial overgeneralisation (e.g. Lévy, 1979) they have made relatively easy targets for criticism. However, a possible 'best case' exception may be found in Glucksmann's 'The Master Thinkers'. In this work Glucksmann has attempted to explore a somewhat broader issue, namely German Idealist philosophy as the source of the fusion of science with the idea of a complete transformation of the social order. The general position outlined in the text is one of opposition to the idea of rational social transformation or construction, on the grounds that an inevitable consequence is the investment of control and domination in the hands of the state.

Glucksmann has argued that for the nineteenth-century German thinkers the French Revolution represented the possibility of a mastery of the social and political universe. The revolution provided clear proof of the effectiveness of thought, of the power of reason to transform the order of things, and in consequence it stimulated a movement away from philosophy and towards science. Glucksmann has stated that science and revolution are closely related, for not only may the latter be regarded as equivalent to a scientific experiment, but, furthermore, 'The enlightenment of science prepares the way for revolution by emancipating the future citizen from that which surrounds him' (1980, p. 140). These statements should not be interpreted as an affirmation of the emancipatory or enlightening benefits of scientific reason; on the contrary, Glucksmann's position seems to be predicated upon a particular interpretation of Foucault's conception of power-knowledge, namely that 'to know is to dominate'. For Glucksmann knowledge is linked to power, to the plans of authority, and to domination, hence his interest in the 'master thinkers' and their authority.

Of the thinkers he has examined Glucksmann has described Marx as the principal master thinker, the most 'operational', the first to systematically advance a programme for 'mastery of the world and of society'. Marx depicted the whole world as ultimately subject to a single system of domination, namely capital, and in so doing he necessarily had to formulate, as a corollary, the view that emancipation would only be achieved through a concerted and centrally organised struggle with capital. Glucksmann has articulated the position as follows: 'only unity of command will put an end to unity of command. The state is needed in order to get rid of the state' (ibid., p. 214). In generating a conception of the existing order as one entirely subject to the power of capital, Marx indirectly placed the possibility of the achievement, or appropriation, of all power on the agenda. If the world was already subject to the dominion of capital, its government through reason merely awaited the seizure of power, the overthrow of the existing authority.

Although Marx was able to anticipate the arrival of that moment at which the power of capital would be smashed, he was relatively silent on prospects for the future. For example, in the 'Critique of the Gotha Programme' Marx refrained from

making any precise comments or recommendations about the
form of life after capitalism. The comments Marx has provided
suggest that, even after the power of capital has been smashed,
people will still be living their lives within the 'narrow horizon
of bourgeois rights'. Glucksmann has made much of this, and
has proceeded to argue that it raises the critical question of
who will take over the 'temporary' responsibility of exercising
the former power of capital (e.g. organising production, etc.),

> who will have a 'sufficiently wide horizon' to be up to the
> level of this historic task? The thinker? The Party? The
> State?.... When the master thinker falls silent, he leaves it
> to the state of the future to differentiate between capitalism
> and communism and to counterpose to the dictatorship of
> private economy its dictatorship of public service. The world
> will belong to the officials. Marx, who was no statist by
> inclination, would have been in despair. (1980, p. 234)

The pessimistic conclusion drawn by Glucksmann is that little
or nothing is to be gained by the substitution of an official for
the capitalist, but that we should not be surprised that this has
happened, for 'masters hand over power only to masters' (ibid.,
p. 235).

Glucksmann's work has received its share of criticism, and in
many respects the criticisms have been warranted. However,
there is less justification for the view that his work, like that
of the other contributors to the 'new philosophy', has been
directed solely towards a critique of Marxism and of the societies
of actually existing socialism. The position outlined by Glucksmann, of the 'rational' state promising freedom but ultimately
delivering tyranny, may indeed apply to the Soviet-type societies embedded in their 'transitional' stage, but it is also apparent
that its applicability extends to the West (cf. Glucksmann, 1980,
pp. 267-9).

In some respects there are echoes in the work of Glucksmann
and other contributors to the 'new philosophy' (e.g. Lévy,
1979) of an earlier non-Marxist position formulated by Max
Weber, in particular an apparent endorsement of the view that
the domination of instrumental forms of rationality constitutes
the destiny of both capitalism and socialism. Furthermore, their
respective analyses have manifested a comparable degree of
pessimism and despair about the future. For the 'new philosophers' there can be no final escape from authority, or from
domination, and therefore the rationale for rebellion or resistance cannot lie with outcomes, or with the achievement of a
final desirable state. Rebellion is not a means to an end, but
rather an end in itself. Thus, for the 'new philosophers',
rebellion has constituted something like an existential act, an
expression of that human residue or potential which has escaped
the disciplinary techniques of reason.

For the 'new philosophers' rebellion and resistance have

assumed diverse forms and have rarely conformed to the patterns prescribed by reason. They have argued that the insurrections, disorders and resistances which have occurred throughout history have always been more complex and diverse than the constructions of the master thinkers have allowed. However, the fact that the conceptions of the master thinkers have not corresponded directly with reality has not constituted a great problem, for as Glucksmann has commented, 'authority's business is, precisely, to make reality bend until it fits the plans' (1980, p. 176).

The work of the 'new philosophers' has elicited a range of critical responses (cf. Debray, 1977; Castoriadis, 1977; Rancière, 1977; Dews, 1979, 1980; Callinicos, 1982). Both Debray and Castoriadis have regarded the interruption of the 'new philosophers' as a dangerous diversion from the pressing social and political questions of the day, namely, 'how to create a new relation between thinking and doing' (Castoriadis, 1977, p. 105), and how to develop an analysis of 'real socialism', and of 'the mechanisms of the domination of man over man, regarding which Marxism falls short' (Debray, 1977, p. 115). Rancière has been similarly dismissive and scornful of the self-proclaimed dissident status of the 'new philosophers', especially because the cultivation of this image has been rewarded with easy access to the mass media. The irony here is that the 'new philosophers' have complained of the plight of Eastern European dissidents (cf. Glucksmann, 1980, p. 69), for whom access to the resources of the media has not generally been available and opposition to the media has constituted one dimension of a general struggle against the domination of the bureaucratic state apparatus, whilst simultaneously dismissing criticism of their own state-regulated mass media as indicative of a contempt for 'ordinary people', to whom the press and television are addressed.

Identifying contradictions, inconsistencies and rhetorical excesses in the works of the 'new philosophers' is not difficult (cf. Dews, 1979, 1980). The thrust of their work has largely been directed towards criticism of Marxism and socialism, the writings of dissidents who have sought to defend and to differentiate Marxism from the existing reality of the Soviet-type societies being conveniently excluded from consideration (e.g. Bahro, Medvedev). Furthermore, their equation of reason per se with domination and the associated description of socialism as the embodiment of technological rationality and tyranny, has led them to reject both science and politics, and to seek solace in aesthetics, religion and metaphysics.

However, beyond the limitations of the work of the 'new philosophers' there lies the enigmatic shadow of Nietzsche, whose work has positive, if as yet barely explored, implications for Marxism (cf. Miller, 1978), and the relatively more sober figure of Foucault, whose work has been influenced by the writings of both Nietzsche and Marx.

4 GENEALOGY, CRITIQUE AND THE ANALYSIS OF POWER

In order to examine the possible implications of Foucault's work for Marxist theory and politics it is necessary to provide an appropriate basis, or context, from which to proceed to consider points of contact, of similarity and of difference, between Foucault's work and Marxist analysis. I do not propose to construct a general summary of Foucault's work, a daunting task which has already been attempted by Sheridan (1980), and in a more modest, critical, and concise fashion by Patton (1979) and Gordon (1979). My reading of Foucault's work, as I hope will become clear, has been structured to a great extent by an interest in the possible implications of his analyses for the key theoretical and political problems at the heart of Marxism. However, the pursuit of this objective requires more than a confinement or subordination of Foucault's work to the unquestioned parameters of historical materialism – a response exemplified by Lecourt (1975) and to a lesser extent by Poulantzas (1978) – but a less than uncritical celebration of that work as somehow constituting a clearly defined and systematic alternative to Marxist theory and politics.

In direct contrast to Marxist theory and analysis Foucault's work does not constitute a form of global theorising; it avoids the reproduction of totalising forms of analysis and is generally critical of systematicity. There is therefore a grave danger in the exercise on which I have embarked of misrepresenting Foucault's work by attributing to it, or imposing upon it, a unity or systematicity to which it is antithetical (cf. Foucault, 1971). However, to acknowledge that Foucault's works do not constitute a system is not synonymous with a denial of their coherence. Although his corpus has a somewhat fragmentary character, and encompasses a variety of apparently disparate topics, there is a clear direction to the work and a strong underlying thematic coherence. For example, Foucault's analyses may be regarded as a contribution to an understanding of the historical conditions of possibility of the human sciences and their social and political effects. His corpus might also be described as pre-eminently concerned with the historical inscription of forms of power on the body, or with the emergence of the 'social' and the modern forms of regulation and administration of populations with which it is concomitant. These formulations are clearly not mutually exclusive, and they may all be incorporated within Gordon's conception of the underlying continuity within Foucault's work, as the analysis or examination of the

relation between forms of rationality and forms of power, or of
the relation between the emergence of particular forms of knowledge and the exercise of specific forms of power.

In examining the relationship of Foucault's work to Marxism it
is important to preserve a sense of proportion, to remember
that the former does not constitute a new 'theory' and that it
does not suggest or authorise a new 'practice'; indeed, it might
be argued that in contrast to the excesses of Althusserian
Marxism, theory is secondary to detailed historical analysis for
Foucault, and further, that a general conception of political
practice is not only absent from his work, but lies beyond its
limits (cf. Gordon, 1979). It is difficult, therefore, to concur
with the judgment advanced by Sheridan: 'Foucault's "political
anatomy" is the clearest and most fully developed version of a
new political "theory" and "practice" that is just beginning to
emerge from the discrediting of both Marxism and "reformism"'
(1980, pp. 221-2). On the contrary, Foucault's work has displayed more of the character of a critique than of an alternative
theory and practice.

The relationship of Foucault's work to Marx and Marxism is
complex and may not be simply reduced, as it seems to have
been by the 'new philosophers', merely to the level of an
opposition or confrontation of ideas. Although Foucault has
been critical of Marxism and has expressed fundamental reservations about the authority invested in the work of Marx, it is
nevertheless evident that the latter has constituted a significant
and positive reference point. An indication of Foucault's
acknowledgment of the significance of Marx's work is present
in several places, but nowhere more so than in the comment:

> It is impossible at the present time to write history without
> using a whole range of concepts directly or indirectly linked
> with Marx's thought and situating oneself within a horizon
> of thought which has been defined and described by Marx.
> (1980a, p. 53)

However, to attribute value to the work of Marx and to acknowledge its continuing influence on the contemporary analysis of
history is not synonymous with an endorsement of attempts to
refurbish historical materialism, perhaps the most notable of
which has been made by Foucault's former teacher and colleague,
Althusser (cf. 1969).

I do not intend to weave my way back along the broken threads
of authorial biography in order to construct an account of
similarities and differences, credits and debits, between Foucault and Althusser, nor do I intend to try to offer a definitive
comparative reading of their texts (cf. Callinicos, 1982). Both
have been described as 'structuralists' and have rejected the
appropriateness or validity of the classification, which is not to
deny that their respective 'early' works may be read in terms
of a critical distancing from existentialism and humanism and

their subsequent analyses in terms of the instructive impact
of the events of May '68 (cf. Poster, 1975; Sheridan, 1980). One
brief observation I do wish to make concerns the ostensibly
common endorsement present in both Foucault's and Althusser's
respective analyses of the idea that Marx was responsible for
the inauguration of the first phase of an epistemological mutation
of history, away from a preoccupation with the sovereignty of
the subject, anthropology, humanism, and uninterrupted continuities, and towards a decentred history, which was characterised by 'analysis of the relations of production, economic
determinations, and the class struggle' (cf. Foucault, 1977c,
p. 13). Beneath this common endorsement there is an important
difference in their respective evaluations of the significance of
Marx's contribution to historical analysis. In Althusser's view
Marx was responsible for an immense scientific revolution which
opened up the continent of history for scientific investigation.·
For Foucault the work of Marx constitutes the source of a new
discursive practice rather than the point of origin of a new
science; furthermore, the work of Nietzsche is identified as
being of equal, if not greater, significance for critical historical
analysis (cf. Sheridan, 1980, pp. 211–18).

Just as the works of Marx have frequently - indeed, necessarily - been interpreted in the light of the significance of
Hegelian philosophy, so the works of Foucault may fruitfully be
explored through a consideration of the import and influence
of the work of Nietzsche. Whether the focus of our inquiry
eventually falls upon the conception and analysis of power-
knowledge relations, the conception of the body as the fundamental or primary material level on which history has been
inscribed, or upon the conception of genealogical analysis, the
presence of a Nietzschean legacy in Foucault's work should
soon become evident.

GENEALOGY AND CRITIQUE

Possibly the simplest and in many respects the most obvious
place from which to begin is with Foucault's conception of history. In a seminal paper - Nietzsche, Genealogy, History
(1977a) - Foucault has expressed his indebtedness to Neitzsche
for an alternative conception of history and historical analysis,
for the conception of genealogy. The conception of genealogical
analysis is differentiated from traditional forms of historical
analysis on several counts. For example, whereas 'traditional',
or 'total', history inserts events into grand explanatory systems
and linear processes, celebrates great moments and individuals,
and seeks to document a point of origin as the source of emana-
tion of a specific historical process or sequence, genealogical
analysis ('effective' or 'general' history) attempts to establish
and preserve the singularity of events, turns away from the
spectacular in favour of the discredited, the neglected, and a

whole range of phenomena which have been denied a history
(e.g. reason, punishment, sexuality). Genealogy rejects the
pursuit of the origin for a conception of historical beginnings
as lowly, complex, and contingent.

In his discussion of genealogical analysis Foucault has made
reference to two interrelated elements: genealogy as the analysis
or examination of descent, and genealogy as the analysis of
emergence. The analysis of descent does not conjure up a
history of uninterrupted continuity; on the contrary, it attempts
to reveal the multiplicity of factors behind an event, to maintain
events in their proper dispersion, and 'to identify the accidents,
the minute deviations ... the errors ... that gave birth to
those things that continue to exist and have value for us' (Foucault, 1977a, p. 146). This emphasis within genealogy is disruptive of traditional historical analyses employing conceptions
of uninterrupted continuities in history: it disturbs the formerly
secure foundations of our knowledge and understanding - not,
however, in order to substitute an alternative and more secure
foundation, but to produce an awareness of the complexity,
contingency, and fragility of historical forms and events to
which 'traditional' history has attributed a stability.

The focus of this element or emphasis within genealogical
analysis appears to fall upon the body - specifically upon 'the
articulation of the body and history'. In this way genealogy as
the analysis of descent establishes that nothing is stable; not
even our nature or physiology escapes the play of historical
forces. As Foucault has observed:

> The body is molded by a great many distinct regimes; it is
> broken down by the rhythms of work, rest, and holidays;
> it is poisoned by food or values, through eating habits or
> moral laws; it conducts resistances. (Ibid., p. 153)

For genealogy as the analysis of descent there can be no constants in history, no essences, no immobile forms, or uninterrupted continuities structuring the past.

The other element of genealogical analysis is concerned with
the examination of emergence, not as 'the final term of an
historical development', but rather as a particular stage in the
struggle or confrontation between forces. Here historical developments are conceptualised merely as transitory manifestations
of relationiships of domination-subordination, as temporary
embodiments of the underlying relationship of forces. The
analysis of emergence, the focus of which is relations of domination, enables genealogy to embrace the confrontations, conflicts, and struggles which produce historical developments
and events. Historical developments are not to be considered
as culminations of historical processes, intentions, or design;
rather they constitute episodic manifestations of series of
subjugations, or temporary manifestations of a stage in the
play of dominations. Genealogy thus conceptualises the emergence

of an event or development as the entry or eruption of forces
for which no subject may be held responsible.

Genealogy, conceived of as the analysis of descent and of
emergence, stands in a critical relationship to traditional history.
Genealogy sets out to reveal the historicity of those qualities
and properties which have formerly been considered ahistorical
(e.g. feelings, sentiment, morality, ideals, the physiology of
the body); it focuses on the discredited, the lowly, on the neglected periods, forms, and events; it 'shortens its vision to
those things nearest to it – the body, the nervous system ...;
it unearths the periods of decadence' (ibid., p. 155); and it
celebrates the perspectivity of knowledge.

Foucault has argued that historians have long since abandoned
events for the extra-historical mechanism or structure to which
the former are subordinated. In contrast, genealogical analysis
has focused upon events, upon singularities. It has set out to
rediscover the multiplicity of factors and processes which have
constituted an event and thereby has sought to disrupt the
self-evident quality ascribed to events through the employment
of historical constants and the ascription of anthropological
traits. Working in the direction of 'eventalisation' requires that
an attempt is made to show that

> things 'weren't as necessary as all that'; it wasn't as a
> matter of course that mad people came to be regarded as
> mentally ill; it wasn't self-evident that the only thing to be
> done with a criminal was to lock him up; it wasn't self-
> evident that the causes of illness were to be sought through
> the individual examination of bodies. (Foucault, 1981a, p.6)

In this way the claim has been generated that genealogical analysis may reveal the several connections, play of forces, and
multiple processes which establish the self-evident intelligibility
of events.

Foucault's reflections on genealogical analysis reveal his basic
commitment to critique, to critical analysis. Such a commitment
is evident in the description of genealogy as giving expression
to subjugated knowledges, as giving voice to histories which
have become lost or neglected within global theoretical systems,
and as rescuing other disqualified forms of knowledge from
ignominy. In particular, genealogical analysis stands in a relationship of opposition to the scientific hierarchisation of knowledges and their effects, its status being that of an anti-science.
However, the focus or object of criticism is not so much the
concepts, methods, and contents of science, as the consequences or effects of 'the centralising powers ... linked to
the institution and functioning of an organised scientific discourse' (1980a, p. 84), in our society.

MARXISM AND SCIENCE

The description of genealogical analysis as standing in a relationship of opposition to the scientific hierarchisation of knowledge provides an appropriate point at which to begin to address
the central issue under examination, namely the relationship of
Foucault's work to the corpus of Marxism. Foucault has addressed the question of the scientificity of Marxism in two ways:
first through a consideration of the emergence and location of
Marx's work within a particular epistemological configuration,
namely that which provided the conditions of possibility for the
emergence of the human sciences in general, and second through
an examination of the power which has accrued to Marxism as a
consequence of the authority associated with its accredited
scientific status.

The first position may be found in 'The Order of Things'
(1973). The focus of this particular text is the epistemological
configuration associated with the emergence of the human
sciences. In the course of an analysis of the formation of the
modern epistemological configuration Foucault has commented
that

> At the deepest level of Western knowledge, Marxism intro-
> duced no real discontinuity, it found its place without dif-
> ficulty ... within an epistemological arrangement that wel-
> comed it gladly ... and that it, in return, had no intention
> of disturbing and, above all, no power to modify, even one
> jot, since it rested entirely upon it. (1973, pp. 261-2)

This controversial observation would appear to be incompatible
with the view that Marx's 'mature' analysis inaugurated an
immense theoretical revolution. Indeed, in so far as Marxism
is depicted as belonging within nineteenth-century thought,
its conditions of existence being synonymous with the emergence
of a specifically modern epistemological arrangement, which, in
turn, Foucault has speculated may be drawing to a close, it is
difficult to sustain the view that Marx's work constituted the
point of emergence of a new science. In addition, such a conception of the epistemological location of Marxism would appear
to undermine an appreciation of its difference from, and opposition to, 'bourgeois' thought.

Subsequently Foucault has expressed some reservations about
his earlier works, describing them as imperfect sketches, and
has acknowledged that Marx revealed an 'entirely new discursive practice on the basis of political economy' (1977c, p. 188).
However, this statement should not be interpreted as signifying
a radical shift of position; on the contrary, it constitutes merely
a qualification which is quite consistent with the position outlined in 'The Order of Things'. Although Foucault has credited
Marx with the introduction of a new discursive practice, he has
simultaneously reaffirmed that it does not constitute a 'trans-

formation of Ricardo's analysis', or represent a new political
economy; it does not, in other words, signify the emergence
of a new science.

I have already implied in my discussion of the conception of
genealogical analysis that Foucault neither claims nor seeks
scientific status for his analyses. An understanding of Foucault's critical distance from scientific discourse may be derived
from a distinction formulated in 'The Archaeology of Knowledge'
between 'scientific domains' and 'archaeological territories'. In
this work it has been argued that the various distinctions
between the major types of discourse (e.g. science, literature,
philosophy, religion, history, fiction, etc.) should not simply
be accepted as constitutive of distinctive unities; rather these
unities should be suspended and their self-evidence inter-
rogated. Thus, discourses, of which the sciences constitute
sub-classes or special cases, become the object of analysis. The
task of analysis becomes the discovery of the conditions within
which specific discourses emerge - what Foucault has termed
their rules of formation. However, although this represents
the general field within which the work may be located, we
should remember that analyses have not been confined to the
discursive alone; of necessity they have embraced the articulation between discursive and non-discursive practices.

It is worth emphasising that the focus of the work is not
confined to the human sciences but encompasses various forms
of knowledge. As Foucault has commented:

> Archaeological territories may extend to 'literary' or 'philo-
> sophical' texts, as well as scientific ones. Knowledge is to
> be found not only in demonstrations, it can also be found
> in fiction, reflexion, narrative accounts, institutional regu-
> lations, and political decisions. (1977c, pp. 183-4)

> What archaeology tries to describe is not the specific struc-
> ture of science, but the very different domain of knowledge.
> (Ibid., p. 195)

Thus all manner of historical documents and dossiers have
been employed in the course of analysis of the conditions within
which discourses have emerged and functioned. Although the
analyses which have been produced since 'The Archaeology of
Knowledge' have continued to explore the conditions within
which discourses have emerged and functioned, there seems to
have been a shift of emphasis towards a more explicit concern
with relationships of power and knowledge, and the effects of
power associated with the scientific hierarchisation of discourses.
This shift is synonymous with the increasing emphasis placed
upon genealogical research by Foucault, upon the importance
of 'the union of erudite knowledge and local memories which
allows us to establish a historical knowledge of struggles and to
make use of this knowledge tactically today' (1980a, p. 83).

Genealogy does not constitute a celebration of error, it does not imply the virtue of intuition or of immediate experience; rather it affirms the importance of critical analysis of 'the scientific hierarchisation of knowledges and the effects intrinsic to their power' (ibid., p. 85). In so far as the history of Marxism may be constructed in terms of a pursuit of scientificity it too falls within the critical terms of reference of genealogy. Therefore, before proceeding to an analysis of the extent to which Marxism constitutes or contains a scientific practice, consideration should be given to the question of the types of knowledge and experience which would be disqualified or excluded on the granting of such a scientific status. The history of Marxist analysis seems to show that each of the different attempts to demonstrate or establish the scientific grounds of Marxism have foundered. But concentrating on this issue misses the point, for an attempt to establish the scientificity of Marxism may well fail to finally or incontrovertibly demonstrate that Marxism has a rational structure, whilst succeeding in 'invest[ing] Marxist discourses and those who uphold them with the effects of a power which the West since Medieval times has attributed to science and has reserved for those engaged in scientific discourse' (ibid., p. 85). This constitutes the source of a second denial in Foucault's work of the radical or alternative character of Marxism. Its pursuit of scientificity has been synonymous with an acceptance of the institutions and the effects of power that invest scientific discourses, or to put the matter in a more familiar form, its embrace of scientificity has been synonymous with the exercise of a form of domination, rather than with a construction of the preconditions for emancipation or liberation. The implication is that genealogy has a better claim to a critical and radical status, for it attempts to give voice to discredited and disqualified forms of knowledge, to promote the insurrection of subjugated knowledges rather than their exclusion or subordination.

At the centre of this contrast between genealogy and scientific discourse there is a conception of power and knowledge relations, or power-knowledge as it has subsequently been formulated. This conception has allowed Foucault to reject the proposition that knowledge is only possible where power relations are suspended and to develop the view that knowledge is not neutral or objective but rather is a product of power relations. In other words knowledge is political in the sense that its conditions of existence or possibility include power relations.

POWER-KNOWLEDGE

The concepts of power and power-knowledge only begin to achieve a prominence in Foucault's work with the appearance of 'Discipline and Punish' and 'The History of Sexuality'. Whether this constitutes a significant break or development in

Foucault's work, or merely an explicit formulation of a theme
that has been present throughout, will probably remain a matter
of conjecture (cf. Patton, 1979, p. 111; Gordon, 1979, p. 23;
Sheridan, 1980, pp. 129-30).

At this point I merely wish to document and to explore, in
general terms, the difference between Foucault's conception of
power and that attributed to or present within Marxist discourse. It has been suggested, somewhat playfully perhaps,
that just as we might credit Freud with having opened up the
continent of sexuality for analysis, so Foucault may be regarded
as having made the exploration of power possible (cf. Donzelot,
1979). Whether this comparison is valid is not at issue here,
although we may wish to affirm the implication of the significance
of the concept of power in Foucault's 'later' writings.

Although a discussion of the mechanisms, relations and effects
of power constitutes a significant dimension in 'The History of
Sexuality', a clearer exposition of the conception of power
introduced by Foucault is to be found in his reflections and
comments on his work. In identifying the question of the exercise of power as the focus of his genealogical analyses Foucault
has argued that the fundamental issue is whether 'the analysis
of power or of powers' may be deduced from the economy. The
thesis is that beneath apparent differences between the juridical-
liberal and Marxist formulations and theorisations of power there
exists a common ground, namely an 'economism in the theory of
power'. In the case of the juridical conception 'power is taken to
be a right', a possession like a commodity. Thus power may be
held, transferred or alienated.

Whilst the Marxist conception differs significantly in some
respects from the juridical conception, there is inherent within
it an assumption of the 'economic functionality of power', power
being conceived principally in terms of 'the role it plays in the
maintenance simultaneously of the relations of production and
of a class domination which the development and specific forms
of the forces of production have rendered possible' (Foucault,
1980a, pp. 88-9). Therefore both the 'juridical' and the Marxist
conceptions of power have been described as in one sense or
another 'economic', in so far as power has been conceptualised
as a commodity, as a possession, or as subordinate to or in
the service of the economy.

Foucault has expressed the view that a non-economic analysis
of power is essential to an unprejudiced understanding of the
interconnection between politics and the economy. Although we
have few alternative conceptions from which to generate different analyses of power, the conceptions of power as exercised,
rather than given or exchanged, and as a relation of force,
rather than as a synonym for 'the maintenance and reproduction
of economic relations', have facilitated the construction of two
alternative non-economic hypotheses. On the one hand there
is 'Reich's hypothesis', namely a conception of the exercise of
power as repression. This is an inherently negative conception

in which power has been depicted as disruptive and limiting, as circumscribing the development of individual creativity or potential. On the other hand there is what Foucault has described as 'Nietzsche's hypothesis', in which power is synonymous with the deployment and expression of relations of force. Foucault has argued that these two hypotheses are linked to the extent that repression might be regarded as the political consequence of the deployment and expression of relations of force, thus together they constitute a schema of domination-repression through which a non-economic analysis of power might be generated.

However, although the latter schema for the analysis of power in terms of relations of force, or domination and repression, may have evaded the 'economism' of the juridical and Marxist conceptions, it is evident that Foucault has come to regard the notion of repression as itself problematic or inappropriate for an understanding of the mechanisms and effects of particular contemporary forms of power.

Foucault's overall project on power may be interpreted as an attempt to invert the traditional mode of analysis 'followed by the entire discourse of right from the time of the Middle Ages'. Concern has not been with the discursive constitution of the legitimacy of power, not with explaining the mechanisms of power through and in terms of the rules of right or the rules of law; rather the focus of the work has fallen upon the reality of domination. Foucault has attempted

> to show not only how right is, in a general way, the instrument of this domination ... but also to show the extent to which, and the forms in which, right (not simply the laws but the whole complex of apparatuses, institutions and regulations responsible for their application) transmits and puts in motion relations that are not relations of sovereignty, but of domination. (Ibid., pp. 95-6)

The sense of domination invoked here is not that of one individual, institution, or class over the people or the nation, but the multiplicity of forms of domination exercised within the fabric of society.

METHODOLOGICAL RULES

Foucault has argued that if the analysis of power is to proceed beyond formulations confined by legalistic conceptions of right, sovereignty, and obedience, to an address of power in terms of domination and subjugation, then specific 'methodological precautions' are necessary. Five such precautions have been proposed concerning the form, level, effect, direction, and 'ideology' of power.

The first methodological rule, constructed in order to avoid an analysis of power in terms of sovereignty and obedience, recommends a 'bracketing' of the regulated, legitimate, and centralised forms of power and a concern instead with 'power at its extremities', with its regional and local forms, where it becomes less legal. The second methodological rule advises that the analysis of power should concentrate not on the level of conscious intention but on the point of application of power, the point at which it is in direct relationship with its object. This methodological rule reduces the significance of questions such as 'Who has power?' or 'What intentions or aims do power holders have?' Foucault has recommended that our interest should be directed to other questions, namely of 'how things work at the level of on-going subjugation, at the level of those continuous and uninterrupted processes which subject our bodies, govern our gestures, dictate our behaviours etc.' (ibid., p. 97). Rather than focus on the issue of the motivation or interest of particular groups, classes or individuals in the exercise of domination, or on the constitution of an all-powerful state or sovereign, attention should be directed to the processes by which subjects are constituted as effects of power.

The third rule or precaution serves to underline the point that power ought not to be conceptualised as the property of an individual or of a class. Power is not possessed or 'appropriated as a commodity or piece of wealth'; rather it has the character of a network, its threads extend everywhere. Thus individuals do not possess power; rather they constitute its effects, 'the element of its articulation ... its vehicle' (ibid., p. 98). To some extent the fourth methodological rule has already been anticipated in the above comments. It emphasises that the analysis of power should proceed from a micro-level, hence the concept formulated by Foucault of a micro-physics of power, and seek to reveal how mechanisms of power have been colonised by more general or 'macro' forms of domination. In other words, the analysis of power should be ascending rather than descending. It is a matter of examining how the techniques and procedures of power operating routinely at the level of everyday life have been appropriated or engaged by 'more general powers or economic interests' rather than the converse, namely of conceptualising power as a property located at the summit of the social order employed in a descending direction over and throughout the entire social domain.

An analysis of the individual mechanisms, histories and trajectories of the micro-powers which then proceeds to a documentation of the manner and method of their colonisation by more global forms of domination is significantly different from analyses which proceed with a conception of power as condensed or located at or within a centre or summit and then seek to track its diffusion, descent, extension and effectiveness throughout society. Conventionally within Marxist discourse power has been conceptualised in the latter form, as ultimately resting with and serving the interests of the bourgeois class and/or the state and as being exercised over and throughout the social domain. According to Foucault we should be wary of such analyses, for 'anything can be deduced from the general phenomenon of the domination of the bourgeois class' (ibid., p. 100). If we are to develop an understanding of power, our efforts have to be directed towards a study of the mechanisms of power and their preconditions, literally towards an analysis of the conditions on which their effectiveness depends.

In Foucault's view the mechanisms, techniques and procedures of power were not formed or invented by the bourgeoisie, they were not the creation of the intentions of a class seeking to exercise effective forms of domination; rather mechanisms, techniques, and procedures of power were adopted or deployed from the moment that they revealed a political and economic utility for the bourgeoisie. Therefore

It is only if we grasp these techniques of power and demonstrate the economic advantage or political utility that derives from them in a given context for specific reasons, that we can understand how these mechanisms come to be effectively incorporated into the social whole. (Ibid., p. 101)

This orientation to analysis allows for an unprejudiced exploration of the grounds on which specific mechanisms, techniques and procedures of power may achieve a degree of economic and political utility for dominant state apparatuses, oligarchies or ruling classes. However, whilst it is evident that there is an acceptance of a possible interconnection between politics and economy, the analysis of power is not reduced to the general terms of reference of a global theory of the capitalist mode of production and its laws of motion or operation. Rather, analysis proceeds under the assumption that there can be no general theory of the connection between power and economic relations, that connections have to be determined through analysis.

The final methodological rule bears directly on the power-knowledge relation and states that the exercise of power is accompanied or paralleled by the production of apparatuses of knowledge. For example, in an analysis of the emergence of one particular type of power, discipline, Foucault (1977b) has argued that the formation of methods and mechanisms of power was synonymous with the constitution of the terrain on which the sciences of man emerged.

These five methodological precautions constitute an invitation to researchers and analysts to study power in terms of its mechanisms, techniques and procedures at its point of application, in its exercise or practice, and to dispense with the juridical-political theory of sovereignty which has exercised a conceptual dominance over analyses of power. The juridical-political theory of sovereign power addressed specific manifestations which Foucault has argued are associated with a feudal type of society, the sovereign-subject relationship being

the fulcrum of the conception of this form of power. With the
advent of new mechanisms of power in the seventeenth and
eighteenth centuries a shift occurred and the theory of sovereignty was displaced, although, as we will see, it has retained
a significant contemporary presence. The theory of sovereignty
addresses general mechanisms of power; it conceives of power
as residing in the sovereign, or as in the case of reactions to
authoritarian and absolutist monarchies, in parliament. In consequence it is inappropriate, indeed inadequate, for an analysis
of a mechanism of power which has effected an increase in the
economic utility and political docility of bodily forces. Such a
mechanism of power,

> which can no longer be formulated in terms of sovereignty
> ... has been a fundamental instrument in the constitution
> of industrial capitalism and of the type of society that is its
> accompaniment. This non-sovereign power which lies outside
> the form of sovereignty, is disciplinary power. (1980a, p. 105)

The conception of disciplinary power, developed in detail in
Foucault's analysis of the birth of the prison (cf. 1977b), will
be discussed below (Chapter 5).

Although it has been argued that a new mechanism of power
emerged in the seventeenth and eighteenth centuries which
began to displace the mechanism of power associated with
sovereignty, this process of change did not involve one mechanism of power succeeding another. The theory of sovereignty
and the associated 'juridical edifice' have not disappeared from
modern societies; rather they have survived and have effected
a form of concealment of the mechanisms of discipline. Furthermore, although the mechanisms of domination through which
disciplinary power has been exercised have been concealed by
the legal enshrinement of a right of sovereignty, these two
dimensions should not be regarded as reality and appearance
respectively, for the theory of sovereignty is not the deceptive
discourse within which discipline, the 'real' mechanism of power,
has operated. Disciplines, as I have already observed, are also
bearers of a discourse, for the exercise of disciplinary power
has been paralleled by the constitution of apparatuses of knowledge. The difference is that whereas from sovereignty a juridical rule has been derived, from discipline and its exercise
a 'natural' rule or norm has been derived. Thus the code which
has emerged from the exercise of disciplinary mechanisms of
power has not been that of law but that of 'normalisation'.

Foucault has suggested that power has been exercised both
through the right of sovereignty and through the exercise of
disciplinary techniques, and he has attempted to demonstrate
that these techniques and their associated discourses have
infiltrated the 'area of right'. One important implication of this
position is the absence of an alternative discourse through
which we might be able to articulate an opposition or criticism

of the effects of power and knowledge associated with the disciplines. The only option open to us has been to express our criticisms of the disciplines and their effects in terms of rights and sovereignty and this has proven counter-productive because, as Foucault has argued, 'sovereignty and disciplinary mechanisms are two absolutely integral constituents of the general mechanism of power in our society' (1980a, p. 108).

The position outlined so far may be briefly summarised as follows. First, an effective criticism of the disciplines and their consequences cannot be articulated through a theory of sovereignty or rights. Second, any critical analysis of power which employs a conception of repression is itself problematic in so far as 'repression remains a juridical-disciplinary notion' (ibid.). Third, the conception of power as repression, constraint, or prohibition is inadequate for an understanding of the contemporary mechanisms through which a positive and productive power is exercised over life.

A RELATIONAL CONCEPTION OF POWER

The text in which Foucault first begins to develop an analytics of power is 'Discipline and Punish' (1977b). In this work a new 'strategical' conception of power is introduced to facilitate an analysis of the relations of power invested in the body. It is not a biological conception of the body which appears in Foucault's work but a historical conception of the body, embedded within a political field, subject to power relations which restrain it, 'invest it, mark it, train it, torture it, force it to carry out tasks, to perform ceremonies, to emit signs' (ibid., p. 25). This Nietzschean conception of the body as inscribed by history and invested with relations of power and domination is the antithesis of conceptions in which the body is the alienated locus of an essential human potential. A negative conception of power as exclusion, concealment or repression, as a force exercised over the body which denies or perverts its 'essence', constitutes the very antithesis of the conception formulated by Foucault. Rather power is conceptualised as productive: 'it produces reality; it produces domains of objects and rituals of truth. The individual and the knowledge that may be gained of him belong to this production' (ibid., p. 194). An additional and no less significant observation which might be made is that power has not been conceptualised as an irresistible force; it may exert pressures but in turn these may be resisted. Subsequently this has lead Foucault to talk in terms of power and resistance. We might note, however, that the conception of resistance within Foucault's discourse has remained as undeveloped as the parallel conception of struggle located within Marxist discourse.

In Foucault's analysis power is not conceptualised as a possession or a privilege; rather it is considered to be exercised through 'dispositions, manoeuvres, tactics, techniques,

functionings'. Power relations are not localised in confrontations
between social classes or between citizens and the state; rather
they are conceptualised as existing at the most elemental level
of the social domain and might be said to constitute it. Reductionist analyses, which locate the source or origin of power and
its effects within a structure or an institution, at a centre or
summit, have been rejected, and instead it has been proposed
that power relations be conceptualised in terms of innumerable
points of confrontation or instability, each of which constitutes
an irreducible event. Such a 'micro-physics' of power may reveal the poverty of political analyses which have assumed the
possibility of overthrowing an existing power, either by seizing
or by destroying the apparatuses through which power, conceptualised as a possession, has been exercised. The possibility
of terminating power, rule, and domination has not only been
a source of inspiration for revolutionary political strategies, but
has also been a cause of their disappointment, for after the
euphoria and hope associated with programmes of fundamental
social change have dispersed, networks of power relations have
tended to re-emerge intact. In contrast Foucault's conception
addresses the presence of power relations in the threshold of
the social order; indeed, its limit point might be considered to
be the equivalence of power relations with sociality itself.

The analysis of power is developed further in 'The History
of Sexuality' (1979a). In this text Foucault has elaborated on
the pervasiveness of the juridico-discursive conception of
power and on its limits and limitations, in particular with
respect to the theorising of new mechanisms of power associated with the development of a political technology of life.

What exactly are we to understand by the juridico-discursive
conception of power? I have already commented on the general
methodological precautions prescribed for the analysis of
power; these receive a more rigorous definition and deployment
in the discussion presented by Foucault on discourses on sex
and sexuality. At the centre of his argument is the view that
there are two dominant explanations of the expression of human
sexuality: one is derived from the repression hypothesis –
desire is repressed or prohibited; the other, which in its turn
is critical of the former position, depicts desire and its expressions as constituted through language, or the act of discourse,
and the concomitant articulation of a rule of law. Now, although
the latter position embodies a partial rejection of the repression
hypothesis by advancing the view that the presence of desire
is already indicative of a power relation and therefore that there
can be no state of desire free from power relations, in other
words no liberation of sexuality from the grip of power, it nevertheless has been argued by Foucault that underlying both
explanations there is a common conception of power. The two
positions are to be distinguished not in terms of a difference
in their respective conceptualisations of power but rather as a
consequence of their respectively quite different conceptions

of the nature and dynamics of sex drives.

A common underlying representation of power is not confined to discourses on sex and sexuality; it is 'deeply rooted in the history of the West' and is present not least of all in political analyses of power. The principal feature of such a conception of power has been identified as that of negation or prohibition:

> it is a power whose model is essentially juridical, centred on nothing more than the statement of the law and the operation of taboos. All the modes of domination, submission, and subjugation are ultimately reduced to an effect of obedience. (Foucault, 1979a, p. 85)

The question which then arises is that of the adequacy and appropriateness of the juridico-discursive conception of power. If we accept that mechanisms of power are not only more complex than the juridico-discursive conception has allowed, but in addition are positive and productive rather than purely negative, how then are we to account for the predominance of the juridico-discursive conception?

Foucault's explanation has been that power is most effective and tolerable when its operations go undetected, when in fact it is possible for individuals to console themselves with the idea of pockets of freedom or limits to power. The emergence of the juridico-discursive conception of power has been associated with the development of monarchical and state institutions in the Middle Ages and their achievement of legitimacy and acceptability through the construction of a regulated order out of a myriad of conflicting power relations. It is at this point, with the formation of a unitary regime, that we might identify the emergence of law as the language of power, if not as an adequate representation of the practice or exercise of power. Although Western monarchies may have engaged in all manner of abuse of rights, Foucault has insisted that, nevertheless, such monarchies 'were constructed as systems of law,... expressed themselves through theories of law, and ... made their mechanisms of power work in the form of law' (ibid., p. 87). However, the juridico-discursive conception is not adequate for the task of analysing the exercise or operation of sovereign power; on the contrary, whilst constituting the sole form of its representation, it has served to occlude the actual practice of power. The juridico-discursive conception has been all that we have known of power; it has been synonymous for us with the exercise and practice of power. Thus, the subterranean operation of other mechanisms of power has passed undetected.

Furthermore, although the power attributed to monarchical and state institutions has been the subject of critical analysis, criticisms have generally remained within the broad terms of reference of the juridico-discursive conception. Critical analyses have tended to assume that the law constitutes the form of power and that power needs must be exercised in the form of

law. Thus the focus of criticism has been upon the point at
which the exercise of power has exceeded the juridical framework, upon abuses and transgressions of the legal code - hence
Foucault's observation that we have been imprisoned within a
mode of conceptualising power that is an embodiment of a
historical form characteristic of a particular period in Western
civilisation. With the emergence of new methods and techniques
of power and their penetration of earlier forms the juridico-
discursive conception has become an obstacle to the development
of an effective analytics of power.

One of the problems associated with Foucault's formulation of
an alternative conception of power is that it has too often been
presented in contradistinction to that which is its antithesis.
We have been informed that power does not refer to institutions
or classes which subordinate the citizens of a state; that it
does not constitute a general system of domination; and that it
is not a legal equivalent to violent subjugation, it does not
represent a form of authority. Indeed, a whole range of phenomena conventionally associated with or invoked as the source of
power (e.g. the state, ruling class, etc.) have been 'bracketed
off' by Foucault. Where a positive conception has been advanced it has taken the form of a description of power as a multiplicity of force relations, as a process, and as a strategy which
may receive institutional embodiment in 'the state apparatus,
in the formulation of the law, in the various social hegemonies'
(ibid., p. 93). Power has been presented as the appropriate
term for the unstable state which emerges from the inequalities
inherent in the highly mobile field of force relations; or to put
the matter more simply, power as a property located in institutions, social positions, or within a social class may be comprehended as the effect of mobile force relations, of the emergent
multiplicity of force relations.

Foucault has denied that power is simply a property or commodity which may be seized or acquired. The conceptual
subordination of power relations to economic, sexual and ideological relationships has been rejected in favour of a conception
which treats power relations as both 'the immediate effects of
the divisions, inequalities, and disequilibriums which occur in
the latter [economic relationships etc.] and [as] ... the internal
conditions of these differentiations' (ibid., p. 94). In addition,
as I have already observed, power is to be conceptualised as
an 'ascending' rather than 'descending' phenomenon, one important consequence of which is that the conception of a global
binary opposition between a ruling class, group or caste and
a ruled or subordinate class or populace at the foundation of
power relations is called into question. Rather than read off
micro-relations of force within the family, at work, and within
other social milieux from a major binary opposition, Foucault has
reversed the direction of analysis and has recommended instead
a conception of major forms of domination as the 'hegemonic effects' which have emerged from the multiplicity of micro-powers.

Two further distinguishing characteristics of Foucault's conception of power should be noted. First, although power is
described as having an objective or aim, it is not the product
of intentionality on the part of a subject. Second, the very
existence of power relations presupposes forms of resistance,
not as an external effect or consequence of the exercise of
power, but as an inherent feature of the power relation. If we
accept the view that where there is power there is resistance,
then it follows that just as power is present everywhere in the
social network so is resistance. Thus broad cleavages in the
social order, massive binary divisions, constitute at best possible fleeting moments in the history of a society amidst a
plurality of irregular resistances. The implication is clear: we
should not assume a 'single locus of great Refusal' for there
are a multiplicity of resistances which are constantly shifting
and regrouping, and a binary division constitutes merely one
possible and exceptional historical form.

POWER OVER LIFE

In developing an analysis of the difference between a juridico-
discursive conception of power and a more appropriate strategical conception, Foucault has argued that the transformation in
the nature of the exercise of power may be regarded as a change
from power as a 'right to *take* life or *let* live' to a form of power
which fosters life, the latter being described as a power over
life, in contrast to the former sovereign power, which has been
described as a power over death. Foucault has argued that the
development of a power over life assumed two basic forms:

(i) an anatomo-politics of the human body
(ii) a bio-politics of the population

The concept of an anatomo-politics of the body refers to those
techniques of power which came to be exercised over physical
or bodily capabilities in order to maximise their economic utility
and political docility. Here we are on the terrain of the disciplines and their effects. The concept of a bio-politics of the
population refers to the second form in which a power over life
developed. In this instance the well-being of the population or
the social body was the object of techniques of power, the focus
of their exercise being the social conditions affecting the biological processes of life (e.g. reproduction, mortality, health,
etc.). The emergence of these respective techniques for sub-
jugating bodies and for regulating populations has been identified by Foucault as marking the beginning of an era of bio-
power, a power over life.
    Foucault's analysis of power-knowledge relations, of the entry
of life 'into the sphere of political techniques' alongside the
development of fields of knowledge which constitute life as their

object, should not be interpreted to mean that life is completely
regulated; on the contrary there has been a constant resistance
to techniques of government and administration. However, a
corpus of knowledge(s), techniques of power, and associated
effects has developed on the basis of a conception of the calcul-
ability and transformability of human life, and it is here that
we may understand the significance of the topic of sexuality for
Foucault, for it is through sex that access may simultaneously
be gained to the 'individual' body and the species body or
population, to the private and to the public domain.

CLASS AND POWER

Although Foucault has not directly addressed the general issue
of Marxist analyses of power, there are references in his work
to conceptions of the exercise of power in Marxist analyses of
sexual repression and class structure which are valuable. Such
references constitute another basis from which to begin to
develop an understanding of the critical implications of the
work for Marxist analysis. For example, Foucault has argued
that a class analysis offers little purchase on the theme of the
deployment of sexuality, for the latter was not established by a
ruling class as a principle of limitation of the pleasures of
others. On the contrary, the technologies of sex were first
deployed within and on the bourgeoisie or ruling classes, the
working classes indeed not being subjected to the deployment
of sexuality until the mid-nineteenth century.
   Rather than endorse a conception of the history of sexuality
as explicable in terms of a mechanism of repression, Victorian
prohibitions ultimately succumbing to twentieth-century liberalisations and permissiveness, Foucault has argued that what we
know as sexuality, that which has been constituted as our
'nature', as the secret of our identity, is in fact the term for
'the set of effects produced in bodies, behaviours, and social
relations by a certain deployment deriving from a complex political technology' (1979a, p. 127). This technology of sex has
constituted a form of surveillance and has operated along the
three axes of pedagogy, medicine, and demography, the object
or target of which, in the first instance, was the bourgeoisie,
'the economically privileged and politically dominant classes'.
Foucault's explanation of this event is that what was at issue
was the maximisation of life, not the sexual repression of
exploited or subordinate classes. What emerged from the exercise of this technology of power has been described as a political ordering of life, a state of affairs which should not be
confused with either a repression of life or a repression of
sexuality. The political ordering of life to which Foucault has
referred is of the order of a culture, the construction of a way
of life, including a cultivation of several dimensions of the
bourgeois body, its hygiene, longevity, reproductive capacity,

protection from diseases and defects.

Foucault has rejected the view, implicitly attributed to Marxist analysis, that the bourgeoisie was responsible for a repression of sexuality or a denial of bodily pleasures, and has instead argued that the technology of sex served in the first instance to constitute a body and a sexuality for the bourgeoisie. By way of an analogy Foucault has described sex as being of equivalent importance to the bourgeoisie as 'blood' to the aristocracy. Just as the aristocracy constructed a sense of its difference, its special qualities, in terms of a concept of blood, 'in the form of the antiquity of its ancestry', so the bourgeoisie sought to affirm the special character of its body through its 'progeny and the health of its organism'. In contrast the working classes suffered living conditions which were indicative of a general lack of concern or recognition for their body and their sex. A concern for the health, longevity and reproduction of the working classes only became an issue with the emergence of conflicts over urban space, epidemics, and diseases; economic developments, in particular the 'need for a stable and competent labour force'; and the establishment of appropriate mechanisms for the surveillance, regulation and administration of the subordinate population. In brief the attribution of a body and a sexuality to the proletariat has been described as synonymous with the process by which the exploited class became an instrument of the bourgeoisie's hegemony.

For Foucault relations of power do not emanate from a sovereign, a state, or a ruling class. The conventional radical conceptualisation of particular manifestations of power relations in terms of the all-encompassing form of state power, which in turn has been interpreted as representing or serving the interests of a dominant class or class fractions, has been rejected because of its neglect of the specificity of power relations. However, the focus of Foucault's analytics of power is not solely, or even primarily, on the production of particular effects at the level of the expressivity or regulation of the body, the individual, or the species arising from the exercise of power. Analysis of the production or emergence of particular discursive formations, notably 'true' discourses, is at least of equal significance, as is evident from Foucault's comment that 'ours is a society which produces and circulates discourse with a truth-function, discourse which passes for the truth and thus holds specific powers' (1980b, p. 4).

For example in the text on sexuality Foucault has discussed the positive mechanisms through which sexualities have been produced. One mode of sexuality discussed by Foucault is that of childhood. On this subject Foucault has argued that the emergence of infantile masturbation as a problem at the beginning of the eighteenth century might be approached through a version of the repression hypothesis, with an argument being constructed along the lines of the dysfunctionality of particular modes of behaviour for the development of capitalism (cf. Reich).

However, to proceed in this manner is to accept a negative conception of power, to imply the existence or presence of a natural
sexuality awaiting release, and to neglect the historical formation of a sexuality specific to childhood. Foucault has argued
that the sexuality of children became a target and an instrument of power as a consequence of changes in the relations
between adults and children, parents and educators, and in
the intensity of internal familial relationships. Childhood became
'the nursery of the population to come' and was therefore identified as being in need of regulation and surveillance. In this
way a power over childhood was established - a power which
was indissociable from the 'true' discourses which were its
corollary, discourses which constructed 'normal' childhood
sexuality and which in turn provided a number of appropriate
positions from which such control and power might be directly
exercised.

Foucault's analyses of power-knowledge relations have sometimes been equated with analyses of ideology; certainly this
has represented one of the methods by which Marxists have
attempted to incorporate selected elements of the work within
a historical materialist frame of reference (cf. Lecourt, 1975).
However, this constitutes a misrepresentation of Foucault's
work, for the concept of ideology, despite the Althusserian
enterprise, has continued to signify the antithesis of 'true'
discourse, in other words error and illusion rather than
'science'. The problem in which Foucault has been interested
is the obverse, namely not the 'economy of the nontrue' but the
'politics of the true'. As I have already indicated, if there is a
positive point of contact with Marxist conceptions it probably
rests with a development of the conception of hegemony formulated by Gramsci (cf. Mouffe, 1979; Mercer, 1980a, 1980b).

FOUCAULT AND MARXISM

Of all the statements and observations in Foucault's work which
represent a direct or indirect criticism of Marxist theory and
politics, those on the Gulag are probably the most controversial
(cf. 1980a, pp. 134-8). Before proceeding to a discussion of
the Gulag question it will be helpful briefly to outline Foucault's
general conception of the relationship between discourses,
practices and effects, for a misunderstanding of the latter relationship may contribute to a misrepresentation of Foucault's
position on the Gulag question.

Three distinct orders of historical events have been differentiated by Foucault, namely discourses, social and institutional
practices, and finally effects which materialise within the social
field. In contrast to the conventional Marxist formulation of
the relationship between theory and practice, in which there
has been a frequent assumption of the possibility of a correspondence, Foucault has conceptualised the relationship

between the orders of discourses, practices and effects as one
of non-correspondence. In turn the existence of a relationship
of non-correspondence between discourses, social and institutional practices and effects has been described as a routine
feature of positive significance requiring analysis in each particular instance. Thus Foucault has indicated that, although the
human sciences and Marxism may indeed construct programmes
for the formation of a social reality, these are not necessarily
translated into appropriate practices and techniques, and
further, even if they do achieve concretisation in the form of
particular social practices then their effective implementation
may itself be regarded as a highly problematic step. In brief,
the normal relationship between discourses, practices and
effects has been one of non-correspondence. This position has
been succinctly expressed by Gordon in the following terms:

> Our world does not follow a programme, but we live in a
> world of programmes, that is to say in a world traversed
> by the effects of discourses whose object (in both senses
> of the word) is the rendering rationalisable, transparent
> and programmable of the real. (1980, p. 245)

Marxism is one such discourse in whose effects Foucault has
been interested. However, it would be a mistake to attribute
to Foucault the view that there is, or has been, a positive
relationship or a direct correspondence between the texts of
Marxist theory and the practice of incarcerating political opponents in penal colonies within the societies of actually existing
socialism.

To avoid such a misrepresentation it is important to clarify
Foucault's conception of the Gulag question. The particular
formulation is significant, for Foucault has not directly addressed the Gulag as an institution, with its own history, functions
and effects, but rather what he has termed the 'Gulag question'. The focus is not the Gulag institution as a form of internment, but rather the strategies through which the Gulag question has been defused within 'Left' discourse. Foucault's
criticism is that the Gulag question has generally not even been
posed, and that when it has been, particular strategies have
been employed to preserve 'the currency ... of a Leftist discourse whose organising principles remain unchanged' (1980a,
p. 137). It has been argued that the following four strategies
have been employed to neutralise the Gulag question:

   (i) theoretical reduction
  (ii) historicist reduction
 (iii) Utopian dissociation
 (iv) universalising dissolution

The first strategy of theoretical reduction has sought to
neutralise the Gulag question by depicting the existence of the

Gulag as a consequence of error, deviation, misrecognition or distortion of the classical texts of the Marxist tradition. If only Marx and Lenin had been interpreted correctly then ... Implicit in this strategy is the notion of a betrayal of the truth of Marxist theory. The second strategy has provided a different answer to the Gulag question, the Gulag being portrayed as a temporary pathology or abnormality, which has to be tolerated as the necessary, if regrettable, price of the development of 'true' socialism, as 'a maternity illness of the country that is painfully giving birth to socialism' (1980a, p. 136). The third type of strategical response has been to treat the presence of the Gulag as an indicator of the existence of pseudo-socialism, as a sign that 'true' socialism has not yet been realised and therefore that the idea or concept of such a possible social form may be protected and preserved from the negative connotations of the Gulag. The final strategy which has been deployed to neutralise the Gulag question has been to argue that Gulags are to be found everywhere (e.g. Latin America, South Africa, South-East Asia, etc.), the corollary of which is that all such forms of confinement must be denounced and criticised. In this way an attempt has been made to reduce the significance of the existence of the Gulag in the societies of actually existing socialism.

Foucault's rebuttal of these strategical responses to the Gulag question has taken the following form. In response to the view that perhaps the classical texts of the Marxist tradition have been misinterpreted or misrepresented and that we may be able to find within them a condemnation of the Gulag he has proposed an alternative, namely an exploration of the texts in order to discover in what way(s) they might have allowed for the Gulag and in what respects they might have served to legitimate its existence. In other words, Foucault has advocated that we should treat the apparent non-correspondence between Marxist discourse and the practices associated with the Gulag in positive terms. Likewise he has argued that instead of examining the Gulag as a pathology we might consider its use, its functions, its place as a 'politico-economic operator in a socialist state'. In response to the third strategy Foucault has demanded that our attention should be devoted not to the difference between Soviet and 'true' socialism but to the reality of the multiple forms of resistance to the Gulag and the circumstances in which people have resisted it. Finally, Foucault has argued that the posing of the Gulag question should indeed be confined to the socialist states, 'in so far as none of these since 1917 has managed to function without a more-or-less developed Gulag system' (ibid., p. 137). This does not represent a denial of the view that Gulags exist elsewhere, but rather constitutes a recognition of the special significance of the societies of actually existing socialism within contemporary radical theory and politics.

Foucault's comments on the Gulag question do not in my view imply a relationship of correspondence between Marxist theory

and the Gulag institution; rather their immediate objective seems
to have been to disrupt the politics of truth of Left discourse,
to challenge the power of Marxist discourse which the strategical
responses outlined above have sought to preserve in the face
of the reality of the Gulag. Posing the Gulag question allows
serious consideration to be given to a range of issues, not least
of which is the controversial matter of the relationship between
Marxist discourse, political practice and its effects.

Poulantzas
There has been a tendency to interpret and to assess the value
of Foucault's work in terms of the fixed parameters of a Marxist
problematic (cf. Lecourt, 1975; Fine, 1979; Lea, 1979). For
example, Lecourt has interpreted the distinction between discursive and non-discursive practices formulated by Foucault as
equivalent to the distinction within Marxist discourse between
the ideological superstructures and the foundation level of the
mode of production – the principal difference noted by Lecourt
being that, whereas within Marxist discourse a general analytical principle of determination has served to order the relationship between 'superstructure' and 'infrastructure', in Foucault's
work a general formulation of the relationship between discursive and non-discursive practices has been absent. Thus Lecourt has commented that Foucault is a theorist of the superstructure, 'condemned to silence over the link between ideology
and the relations of production' (1975, p. 207).
    There are several problems with Lecourt's interpretation, and
most of them emanate from the attempt to subordinate Foucault's
analysis to an unquestioned Marxist analysis, and the concomitant neglect of radical differences between the two modes of
analysis. Foucault has sought to reveal the rules of formation
of discourses (systems of formal statements about the world)
and to analyse their articulation with and regulation by non-
discursive practices (social and institutional practices). In each
instance the relationship between discursive and non-discursive
practices has been subjected to analysis rather than submitted
to a preordained principle of determination. In contrast, for
Lecourt, the relationship between 'discourses' and the 'world'
or discourse and reality has been conceptualised in terms of
two assumptions: first of the adequacy of the Marxist principle
of economic determination, and second of the possibility of a
close correspondence between discourse and reality. Foucault's
analyses have challenged not only the conception of a general
theory of the relationship in question but, in addition, both
the master principle of economic determination and the conception of a correspondence between discourses, practices and
effects.
    A qualitatively different response – what might be termed more
of a critical appreciation – is to be found in the work of Poulantzas (1978). Although there are good grounds for regarding the
work of Poulantzas as unrepresentative (cf. Hall, 1980),

especially in so far as it has displayed a readiness to critically
engage with 'the licensed guardians of Marxist dogma who refuse
to see that there is any problem with Marx's theory itself' (1978,
p. 112), it constitutes possibly the best example to date of an
exploration of the implications of Foucault's work for Marxist
theory and politics, and is therefore worthy of closer examination. The focus of my discussion will be on this one particular
feature of Poulantzas's work, namely his response to Foucault's
project as, on the one hand, a resource for addressing and
possibly resolving some of the problems and limitations of
Marxist theory and, on the other hand, the source of an alternative and challenging problematic which needs to be subjected
to criticism. This dual reference to Foucault's work as the
source of new positive insights and yet as an appropriate target
for criticism is to be found in Poulantzas's 'State, Power,
Socialism' (1978), the focus of which is the relationship between
the state, power and social class.

The text commences with a series of cryptic observations on
traditional representations of the state and relations of power
within political theory in general and Marxism in particular. The
basic proposition from which the text proceeds is that the state
exhibits 'a peculiar material framework that can by no means
be reduced to mere political domination' (1978, p. 14). Hence we
are informed that the institutional materiality of the state ex-
ceeds the exercise of state power, and that the state is neither
the construction of a ruling class nor simply there to be appropriated. In developing an analysis of the institutional materiality
of the state and relations of power, Poulantzas has commented
that the basis 'has to be sought in the relations of production
and social division of labour'. This does not mean a return to
the conventional Marxist topographical metaphor of 'base' and
'superstructure', for Poulantzas has rejected the conception
of the state as an epiphenomenon of the economy along with the
alternative conception of the state as an autonomous 'superstructural instance'. Both positions, the former employing the
base-superstructure metaphor and the latter a conception of
the social totality in terms of instances or levels, ultimately
assume the possibility of a general theory of the economy and
in addition conceptualise the state-economy relationship as one
of exteriority.

In contrast Poulantzas has stated first, that the relationship
between the state and the economy is not one of externality,
where the state intervenes in the economy, for '*The political
field of the State ... has always, in different forms, been present in the constitution and reproduction of the relations of
production*' (ibid., p. 17). Second, he has stated that there
can be no general theory of the economy and that a general
theory of the state is similarly inadmissible, for the theoretical
objects of economic analysis and political science or sociology
do not remain constant, and are not in any case subject to their
own specific laws of transformation. Thus Poulantzas has con-

cluded that 'no general theory of the State [is] to be found in the Marxist classics' (ibid., p. 20), because such a theory is not possible. At best we may attempt to construct a regional theory of the capitalist state – a possibility which arises from the existence of particular historical conditions, namely the distinctiveness or separateness of the state and the economy in the capitalist mode of production.

It is evident that Poulantzas has two targets in sight. To begin with he has sought to undermine the view that *'general theoretical propositions concerning the State'*, which may be found in the classical texts of the Marxist tradition, constitute the basis on which a general Marxist-Leninist theory of the state may be fabricated. In addition, he has simultaneously attempted to neutralise the criticism that Marxism lacks a general theory of power, politics, or the state. The implications of the introductory comments are extensive, perhaps the most significant being that, if it is not possible to formulate a general theory of the state, then it necessarily follows that a general theory of the transition from one state form to another is similarly out of the question. This means that there cannot be a general theory of the transition from capitalism to socialism. At best we are left with the possibility of a theory of the capitalist state from which we may generate insights about a transition to socialism. However, any such propositions about a transition to socialism will have an ambiguous status, for 'They can never be anything other than *applied theoretical-strategic notions*, serving to be sure, as guides to action, but at the very most in the manner of road-signs' (ibid., p. 22).

Admission of the fallibility of our knowledge and of the un-avoidable absence of a model of the transition to socialism has constituted the context in which Poulantzas has found it necessary to refer directly to the problematic relationship of theory and practice, to offer a general observation on the inevitability of a gap existing between theory and practice, theory and the real, and a specific criticism of the position advanced by the 'new philosophers', namely that there is indeed a relationship of correspondence between Marxist theory and the practices of the socialist states in Eastern Europe, or in other words that Marxism may be held responsible for the totalitarianism evident in Eastern Europe. The position out-lined by Poulantzas is that there will always be a distance between theory and practice, theory and the real, and that it therefore makes no sense to hold Marxism responsible for the events in Eastern Europe.

Poulantzas's position on the distance between theory and practice, described as overlapping that between theory and the real, seems to parallel the conception present in Foucault's work of a relationship of non-correspondence between dis-courses, practices and effects. It is clear that the distance or gap between theory and practice, theory and the real, is not a temporary phenomenon which will be transformed by the resur-

rection of a politicised labour movement, neither is it a product
of the dissipation of a revolutionary class; rather it constitutes
a feature of any theory, not just Marxism. In other words no
promise can be extended that the gap may be closed; on the
contrary the impression is conveyed that it is just such a mistaken conception that has constituted the ground on which has .
arisen the association of Marxism with totalitarianism. Thus, for
Poulantzas, Marxist theory does not constitute a resource from
which might emerge 'an infallible formula, purged of all deviations, with which to ensure a genuine transition to democratic
socialism' (ibid., p. 23).

In his introductory comments Poulantzas has proposed that
the relationship of the state with social classes and class struggle should be conceptualised primarily in terms of the 'state-
relations of production' nexus, the relations of production being accorded primacy over the labour process (the forces of
production, technology or technical process) within the production process. The concept of relations of production employed
by Poulantzas includes political and ideological relations – relations which are 'present in the constitution of the relations of
production'. Thus the idea that 'exterior' political and ideological relations merely reproduce the social relations of production has been rejected, and in its place a conception has been
inserted of politico-ideological relations as already present in
the actual constitution of relations of production. This conception enables us to understand the basis on which politico-
ideological relations have played such a significant part in the
reproduction of relations of production. It provides the necessary means for theorising the role of the state in the constitution and reproduction of the relations of production 'as the
factor which concentrates, condenses, materialises and incarn-
ates politico-ideological relations in a form specific to the given
mode of production' (ibid., p. 27). Furthermore, just as the
relations of production are not exterior to or prior to political
and ideological relations, so in turn they are not external to
power and class struggle. Indeed, class powers, concretised
and legitimated in political and ideological relations, constitute
the necessary expression of the relations of production. Thus
the position outlined by Poulantzas is that the relations of
production may not be conceptualised independently of social
classes, which in turn have no existence outside of relations of
power and struggle. The upshot of this is that an analysis of
the 'state-relations of production' nexus requires an analysis
of the presence of the state in the social class struggle, with
the proviso that such an analysis should not remain confined
within a negative, juridical conception of the state and relations
of power, that is to say a conception of the efficacy of the state
restricted to the exercise of domination through ideological and
repressive apparatuses.

To circumvent such a negative conception of state power,
Poulantzas has drawn upon Foucault's analysis of positive and

productive powers. However, although he has sought to formulate a conception of the institutional materiality of the state and
relations of power which is not circumscribed by a Gramscian-
Althusserian conception of the state functioning purely in
terms of repressive and ideological apparatuses, Poulantzas has
not rejected this more conventional conception. Indeed, there
is a reaffirmation of the fundamental significance of force and
violence for the establishment and maintenance of power and,
in addition, an endorsement of the conception of the state's
presence within ideological institutions. The distinctive feature
of the position outlined by Poulantzas is that it constitutes an
attempt to construct a conception of the institutional materiality
of the state and relations of power which extends beyond the
restrictive limits associated with a conception of the efficacy
or function of the state in terms of 'repression plus ideology'.
The implication is that we should recognise that the activities
of the state extend far beyond repression and ideology and
develop analyses and concepts accordingly, for the representation of the state in terms of repression and ideology has served
to obstruct the development of an understanding of its positive
and productive capacities, in particular the construction of a
material substructure of measures and benefits of positive significance and value for the community in general.

In responding to the issue of the state and relations of power
within Marxism, Poulantzas has confronted three dilemmas: the
relative neglect of analysis of the state arising from the tendency towards economism; the form which the response to this
neglect or absence has taken, namely a concentration on the
theorisation of the superstructures, focusing in particular upon
the extensive activity and role of the state, which in turn has
precipitated accusations of 'statism'; and finally the danger
that in attempting to chart a course around economism and
statism, analysis may depart from the central tenets of a
Marxist problematic – a resolution of the problem of power may
take us beyond Marxism.

As the analysis of the institutional materiality of the state and
relations of power develops in 'State, Power, Socialism', so the
influence of Foucault's work becomes more evident. We are
informed that the state constitutes the site of the production of
several discourses and that there is an inextricable relationship
between the state's production of knowledge, techniques of
knowledge, and its exercise of power. It is at this point that
Poulantzas has proceeded directly to the question of the locus
of power and to an assessment of particular aspects of Foucault's
work which bear on the question of power and, to a lesser
extent, that of the state, the object of the exercise being the
construction of an analysis of power and the state which avoids
the pitfalls of both 'statism' and 'economism'.

Poulantzas has argued that power extends beyond the sinews
of the state, and a corollary of this is that class powers may
not be reduced to the state and its respective apparatuses.

However, this does not mean that the state is relegated to a
secondary level or position; on the contrary, we are advised
that the state plays a constitutive role in the relations of production and the class struggle. Furthermore, to emphasise the
point, Poulantzas has stated that '*In the order of theoretical
explanation*; it makes no sense whatever to speak of a social
field of class division of labour and class power existing *prior*
to the State' (ibid., p. 39). In other words, class struggle is
not to be conceptualised as the origin of the state, for from the
outset, within a class-divided society, the state constitutes a
necessary structure. Indeed, Poulantzas has commented that
the very intelligibility or knowledge of social reality, whose
history has been conceptualised within Marxism as the history
of class struggles, is inconceivable without the presence of
the state.

However, whilst presenting an argument which at times begins
to edge towards 'statism', the sinews of the state seeming to
stretch throughout the social network, Poulantzas has, simultaneously, attempted to retain the proposition that relations of
power extend beyond the state, and in addition to reaffirm both
the proposition that the relations of production exercise a
determining role and the proposition that class struggles have
a primacy over the state. Now, we may accept that the references here to determination and primacy refer to an analytical
priority rather than to a historical precedence, whilst nevertheless suspecting the re-emergence of an old problem, namely
economism.

Although Poulantzas has referred to political and ideological
relations as legitimising, consecrating and being present in
economic relations, and in turn has noted that 'relations of
production are already relations of struggle and power' the
bottom line remains that 'relations of production still play the
determining role' (ibid., p. 45). Furthermore, whilst accepting
that power relations may extend beyond class relations, Poulantzas has argued that given a class-divided society it necessarily follows that the state acts as a mechanism through which
all relations of power are assigned a class pertinency. Therefore, even though it has been acknowledged that power relations extend beyond class relations and, in addition, that power
reaches beyond the network of the state, Poulantzas has finally
reaffirmed the proposition that 'Class power is the cornerstone
of power in class divided social formations' (ibid., p. 44), and
has argued that in the capitalist mode of production (political)
'power is pre-eminently concentrated and materialised by the
State, which is thus the central site of the exercise of power'.

The principal positive feature of Foucault's work for Poulantzas is its provision of a materialist analysis of particular institutions of power. Foucault's work, or rather aspects of it, may
be considered compatible with Marxist analyses of the state in
so far as insights are generated into the process of individualisation, that is the establishment or forging of individuality

through the process of normalisation. Foucault has thus been credited with having theorised the process by which individuality is constituted through a network of power-knowledge relations directed at the human body and psyche. However, whereas for Foucault the focus of analysis is the mechanisms and effects of the exercise of power, power relations being conceptualised as rooted deep in the social network rather than in economic conditions, for Poulantzas the materiality of power is rooted in the relations of production and the social division of labour. Furthermore, although Poulantzas has accepted that relations of power may not be simply reduced to class relations, that 'class division is not the exclusive terrain of the constitution of power', he nevertheless has reasserted that the 'institutional specificity of modern power' is grounded in the 'economic'. There is therefore a clear tension between Poulantzas's admission that power relations are dispersed throughout the social body and his reiteration of what is ultimately a conventional, if sophisticated, Marxist position, namely that the state has an essential class nature and in addition penetrates other power relations.

This tension or contradiction in Poulantzas's analysis is a product of an attempted incorporation of elements of Foucault's work. It is a symptom of a significant degree of incompatibility between Foucault's genealogical analyses and Marxist analysis. Nevertheless, there are benefits to be derived from the exercise in which Poulantzas has been engaged – benefits specifically in the area of political strategy (cf. Minson, 1980). Reflecting on the proposition that relations of power may not be reduced to class relations draws attention to the tendency within Marxism to subordinate all forms of struggle to the only level deemed politically significant, namely that of class struggle. Once it is accepted that non-class struggles have an autonomous existence, then the nature of political struggles and alliances assumes a fresh significance. A corollary of this is that it reminds us that the continued existence of relations of power within the societies of actually existing socialism in Eastern Europe is not a sign of abnormality or of a 'temporary' delay; rather it indicates that relations of power are not eliminated merely by a proletariat or a party taking control of the state. On both counts Marxist strategies for socialism are called into question (cf. Minson, 1980).

Reprise – on the question of a relational theory of power
Whilst Poulantzas has acknowledged the partial correctness of Foucault's strategic conception of power, has endorsed the view that power is not an institution, a structure, or 'a certain might with which some are endowed', and has confirmed the proposition that *'the field of power is ... strictly relational'*, it is also evident that significant differences remain between their respective positions.

The most fundamental difference is that within Marxist analysis power always has a precise basis and in the paradigm case of class division and struggle it basically takes the form of exploitation; the location of the respective social classes in the 'various power apparatuses and mechanisms'; and the state apparatus. In contrast, for Foucault, power relations, relations of force, are themselves the very basis, the fibre or network, of the social domain; they are synonymous with sociality. In responding to this position Poulantzas has argued that Foucault is thereby trapped within a 'logical impasse', namely that, given such a conception of power, there can be no escape, no locus of opposition or resistance, because power itself has no specific basis or ground. Proceeding along these lines Poulantzas has added that the concepts of power and resistance in Foucault's work are 'equivalent poles of a relation', and further, that it is the power pole which has been accorded primacy. This is fair comment in so far as Foucault's analyses have indeed focused on the relationship between forms of rationality (knowledge) and forms of power to the detriment of the question of forms of opposition and resistance. However, the absence of the latter in Foucault's work is not necessarily a sign of fatalism, or of a conception of the inevitability of domination. Indeed, we might agree that Foucault has neglected analysis of forms of resistance and opposition, but regard such an omission as no different in principle from the comparable neglect within Marxism of analysis of forms of struggle. Given that we do not deduce from the latter that the inevitable fate of class struggle and conflict is institutionalisation and neutralisation, there would seem to be no warrant for attributing a fatalistic position to Foucault.

Poulantzas has criticised Foucault for not recognising that power is grounded in the relations of production, arguing that 'the power of a class refers above all to its objective place in economic, political, and ideological relations' (1978, p. 147), with determination resting at the level of economic relations. Likewise, resistance or opposition have been conceptualised as rooted in the exploitative structure of the relations of production, class struggle being the basis of resistance. Now there are three observations I wish to make on these specific responses to Foucault's analysis. First, Poulantzas's partial endorsement of Foucault's relational theory of power is not without ambiguity. Specifically it has led Poulantzas to attempt to translate Foucault's analyses of the exercise of power, power as a multiplicity of force relations, into class terms, the outcome being several formulations which, although making reference to a relational conception of power, continually invoke conceptions of power as possession, property, or capacity. For example, Poulantzas has stated that 'applied to social classes, power should be understood as the capacity of one or several classes to realize their specific interests' (ibid., p. 147), and even though this statement is qualified in terms of a recognition that interests are realised in a relational field of opposing classes, and that, in turn, capacity is derived from the objective location of a social class, the sense persists that although its derivation may be complex and its nature not that of a quantum, nevertheless power may be conceptualised as the property or possession of a class. At least that is the implication of references to the 'political power of a class', 'the place of each class and hence its power', and other comparable formulations.

Poulantzas does not follow through the implications of Foucault's relational theory of power; rather the conception of power as the 'multiplicity of force relations immanent in the sphere in which they operate' (Foucault, 1979a, p. 92) is redefined in terms of one form of relation, namely class relations, which are then accorded primacy. Thus Poulantzas has argued that all struggles, including non-class struggles, acquire their meaning 'only to the extent that class struggles exist and allow other struggles to unfold' (1978, p. 148) - which brings us back to the question of opposition and resistance and my second observation.

I am not unsympathetic to the view that Foucault has been overly preoccupied with the question of power to the detriment of the question of resistance (cf. Gordon, 1980). However, the criticism outlined by Poulantzas, namely that in Foucault's work there is no escape from domination since resistance is always inscribed within power, is predicated upon a clear misunderstanding. Ironically, Foucault has addressed this very misunderstanding in the following rhetorical fashion:

> Should it be said that one is always 'inside' power, there is no 'escaping' it, there is no absolute outside where it is concerned, because one is subject to the law in any case? (1979a, p. 95)

The answer given is that to do so would be to misunderstand the relational character of power, power relationships being dependent upon the existence of a multiplicity of points of resistance. Thus Foucault has argued that relations of force require opposition or resistance and that these are present throughout the network of power relations. In other words, there is no single necessary locus or source of opposition; rather there are a plurality of resistances which 'can only exist in the strategic field of power relations'. However, this does not mean, as Poulantzas has implied, that resistance is 'doomed to perpetual defeat'; on the contrary it constitutes the irreducible opposite of power relations and may take many forms, the comparative effectiveness of which has yet to be subjected to critical analysis. This brings me to my final observation.

The emphasis in Foucault's work has been on an unprejudiced examination of the complex mechanisms through which power has functioned. The exercise of power and the mechanisms through which it has functioned have been conceptualised neither as autonomous of nor as subordinate to economic processes and relations of production. Foucault has not denied that local struggles against power may be related to struggles against

economic exploitation (cf. 1977a, p. 216), but has argued that
the exercise of power and the mechanisms through which it is
effective may not be theorised or accounted for in terms of
capitalist exploitation and relations of production. An analysis
of the mechanisms through which power is exercised, and of
the relationships between struggles against powers and struggles against exploitation, may not simply be derived from an
existing totalising theoretical system. Such mechanisms and
relationships need to be analysed in their own right as 'events',
rather than subordinated to existing conceptions of global
historical processes which have proven to be far from infallible.

Finally I should like to turn to the question of the state. I
have already noted that Foucault's work has been described as
being of some value in so far as it illuminates the processes of
individualisation and normalisation – processes conceptualised
by Poulantzas as organised and conducted essentially by the
state. I will address in some detail the issue of normalisation
and Foucault's discussion of the technologies of power, the
'disciplines', associated with this process in the following essay.
However, before concluding, there are a few additional appropriate observations which I would like to make on the criticisms
of Foucault's work advanced by Poulantzas.

Poulantzas has suggested that not only has Foucault under-
estimated the significance of social class and class struggle but
in addition he has neglected the importance of the state at the
very time when its expansion and weight are 'assuming propor-
tions never seen before'. Thus a battery of charges have been
levelled at Foucault's work on power, most notably that it
reveals on overly narrow conception of the state limited to the
public apparatuses of the army, the police, prisons, courts
and so forth, and that in consequence it has neglected a number
of other sites of state power (e.g. the apparatus of asylums and
hospitals, and the sports apparatus). The implication is that
Foucault's conceptualisation of power relations extending beyond
the sphere of the state is the product of an erroneously restrictive concept of the state. This is more than a little ironic, for
the position adopted by Poulantzas itself requires the conceptual
means to theorise power relations 'beyond' the state, otherwise
the criticism of Marxism embodied in Foucault's work, namely
that it has consistently conceptualised power in the form of
state power, will be sustained. The route by which Poulantzas
has sought to avoid this impasse is through the qualification
that even though the contemporary state has maximised the
concentration of power and has intervened increasingly in all
spheres of social reality, nevertheless, 'class powers ... still
stretch beyond the State'. This is a familiar position; it represents a return to base, a return to the premise of the primacy
of class relations and struggle.

In this way Poulantzas has diluted the radical and critical
potential of Foucault's work. The materiality of power, the
mechanisms through which it has been exercised and deemed

effective, have been conceptualised by Poulantzas as synonymous with, or at least reducible to, the operation of the state.
By invoking the state as the point of confluence of power the
specific terms of reference of Foucault's work have been dis-
torted and the important conceptual distinction between general
mechanisms of state power and other, more individualising forms
of power (e.g. forms of power exercised within the family) has
been lost. Although Poulantzas has acknowledged that relations
of power extend far beyond the state, in the final instance such
relations have been ambiguously conceptualised in terms of class
relations.

Ultimately for Poulantzas the very foundation of power seems
to lie with the repressive state apparatus (the army, police,
judicial system), with the means for exercising violence. Thus,
although Foucault has been credited with revealing 'the materiality of the techniques for exercising power', he has been criticised for neglecting the role of law and physical repression
in the functioning of the state. Besides being critical of the
thesis that the exercise of power in modern societies has taken
quite novel and less overtly violent and repressive forms (e.g.
'disciplines', bio-power), Poulantzas has mounted a criticism
of analyses which have suggested that modern forms of power
are grounded in the organisation or manipulation of consent
rather than in the use of physical violence (e.g. the Frankfurt
School). Both positions have been criticised for underestimating
'the role of violence in grounding power' (1978, p. 79).

The violence-terror referred to by Poulantzas as the ground
of power is the monopoly of the state, it

permanently underlies the techniques of power and mechanisms of consent: it is inscribed in the web of disciplinary
and ideological devices; and even when not directly exercised, it shapes the materiality of the social body upon which
domination is brought to bear. (Ibid., p. 81)

In brief, Poulantzas has criticised Foucault's conception and
analysis of power for absorbing the question of physical violence
and for neglecting the question of consent. On the first point
it is evident that Foucault has placed emphasis upon the significance of the emergence of new mechanisms of power which
are considered to have displaced the violence-terror associated
with the exercise of sovereign power, the argument being that
the exercise of power has become more 'economical', less prone
to the excesses of violence-terror. It is worth emphasising that
Foucault has not spoken of the disappearance of Sovereign-Law,
but rather of its infiltration and transformation by the emergence of new mechanisms of power. On the second point Poulantzas is correct: Foucault does not directly address the issue of
consent. However, a concept of consent would in any case be
inappropriate, for it signifies a relation between subjects, and
it is the issue of the formation of the subject, or more precisely

historical analysis of the different modes by which human beings are made subjects, which has constituted a persistent underlying theme in Foucault's work (cf. 1977b, 1982). Foucault does not so much neglect the question of consent as attend to a fundamental precondition, namely analysis of the particular modes by which human beings become subjects.

Although there are substantial differences between the type of analysis conducted by Foucault and a Marxist analysis, the distance between the two positions is not entirely of the order outlined by Poulantzas. Although an analysis of the state is indeed absent from Foucault's work, this reflects the decision to analyse the development of modern techniques of power which may not be reduced to the form of the state. It does not signify a denial of the existence of state power, rather that 'For the State to function in the way it does, there must be, ... quite specific relations of domination which have their own configuration and relative autonomy' (Foucault, 1980a, p. 188).

Foucault's approach to the study of power may be different from that which has been endorsed by Poulantzas, but we should avoid exaggerating the differences. Foucault has recommended an 'ascending' analysis of power, the focus being upon the new mechanisms of power which have penetrated the body and everyday existence. Although this approach may be regarded as the antithesis of that formulated by Poulantzas, in so far as the implication is that state power is constructed and functions on the basis of particular micro-powers, it is also apparent that such powers are not autonomous or independent, but are inextricably associated with a series of broad historical processes of which economic processes constitute a part. Foucault may not have prioritised the analysis of state power or have affirmed the conception of economic determination in the final instance, but neither has he argued that there are no general mechanisms of state power, nor that there is no relationship between relations of power and relations of production. Indeed, Foucault has made several references to the economic dimensions of the conjuncture within which disciplinary mechanisms of power emerged, and in addition has acknowledged the existence of general mechanisms of state power and their interlocking relationship with other 'micro' forms of power (cf. 1977b, 1980a, 1981b, 1982). The significant difference between the two positions is that for Foucault it is no longer feasible to conceptualise relations of power, and the associated mechanisms and effects, simply in terms of the state, class struggle, relations of production and capitalist exploitation. Power has to be analysed in all its diverse forms, in its exercise, rather than solely in terms of the most centralised possible institutional locus.

5   DISCIPLINE AND SOCIAL
REGULATION

In exploring the political rationality of our present, Foucault has differentiated between two developments, namely an increasing centralisation of political power in the form of the state, and the emergence of technologies of power oriented towards individuals, with the emphasis being placed on the latter, on the study of individualising forms of power.

The decision to concentrate upon individualising technologies of power reflects Foucault's view that conceptualising the exercise of power in terms of the organisation of the state has had undesirable analytical and political consequences. Analytically it has precipitated a neglect of individualising forms of power, the emergence of new technologies of power having been obscured by the focus upon the state. Politically it has led revolutionary movements to constitute themselves in the image of the state, to seek to accumulate comparable politico-military forces, and to adopt hierarchical and bureaucratic forms of organisation, the corollary of which has been that a state apparatus has been deemed integral to the successful negotiation of a post-revolutionary 'transitional' period. Thereby revolutions have been undermined, one state form being replaced by another 'with the same objectives and the same effects' (1981b, p. 254). In contrast the position adopted by Foucault is that

> power isn't localised in the State apparatus and that nothing in society will be changed if the mechanisms of power that function outside, below and alongside the State apparatuses, on a much more minute and everyday level, are not also changed. (1980a, p. 60)

Hence the importance of a conception of 'the social' in Foucault's work, the domain in which positive, productive, local, and individualising forms of power have emerged and been exercised.

Foucault has made reference to specific events and transformations which occurred in the seventeenth, eighteenth, and nineteenth centuries, in particular to a process of reversal of the 'axis of individualisation', away from accounts and celebrations of powerful individuals (e.g. the sovereign), which constituted an 'individuality of the memorable man', towards the collation of files, records, documents, and information on common individuals on and over whom power was to be exercised, thereby effectively constituting an individuality of the 'calculable man'. This transformation was synonymous with the emergence and elaboration of new forms of the exercise of power, specifically techniques for the formation and administration of individuals and for the regulation of the social, which in turn were inextricably associated with the emergence of new 'rationalities', new forms of knowledge, the human sciences. Implicit here is a conception of the necessary interdependence between relations of power and forms of knowledge, a conception of power-knowledge relations.

DISCIPLINE

Foucault first began to explicitly address the question of power in his book 'Discipline and Punish' (1977b). Although the immediate focus of this work is on the power to punish and the institution of the prison, my comments will largely be confined to the broader question of discipline as a general formula of domination, and to the event described by Foucault as the emergence of a disciplinary society.

In his discussion of changes in the form of punishment and the function of the prison Foucault has argued that the shift of focus from the body as the immediate and direct target of the exercise of power (punishment) to 'the soul' or 'knowable man' conceptualised in terms of psyche, subjectivity, personality, consciousness, and individuality was a product of the emergence of new forms of power and concomitant new forms of knowledge. The inference here is not that of a liberating process in which the body is released from the tyranny of power, but rather of a fundamental and positive transformation involving the emergence of a new technology of power, discipline, and the production through the exercise of this new form of power of a new reality and knowledge, that of the individual.

The development of discipline signified the emergence of a new form of power. Whereas the system of power, associated with the sovereign and sovereignty, was spectacular, ritualistic, visible, and manifestly violent, and consequently weighed very heavily on the population, producing fears that reaction in the form of cycles of perpetually reinforced resistance would ultimately destabilise the social and political order, the new tactics of power defined by discipline were qualitatively different, being subject to the following criteria. First, the exercise of power was to be obtained at the lowest possible cost: in economic terms this meant low expenditure, and in political terms it meant that power was to be exercised discreetly in order to reduce the likelihood that resistance would be aroused. Second, the impact, intensity, and extent of the effect of power was to be maximised without interruption. Third, the 'economic' growth of power was to be linked with 'the output of the apparatuses (educational, military, industrial or medical) within which it is exercised' (1977b, p. 218).

It was in the course of the eighteenth century that discipline
- the methods of observation, recording, calculation, regulation,
and training to which the body had long been subjected in
monasteries, armies, and workshops - became a general formula
of domination. The principal reference of disciplinary power has
been 'the whole indefinite domain of the non-conforming'; its
objective, the regulation and ordering of human multiplicities,
within which the process of individualisation - the formation and
control of individuals through training and normalisation - has
constituted a central feature. Discipline has comprised a set of
techniques: the decomposition of multiplicities into units, and
units into component elements (e.g. groups into individuals,
processes into practices, undifferentiated spaces into 'individual' units suitable for surveillance, actions into movements,
etc.); the regulation and optimal development of bodily potential
(viz. the production of utility/docility); the construction of a
social network of visibility (the eye of authority) which would
maintain individuals in their subjection; and a recomposition of
multiplicities or units in order to optimise performance (e.g. as
in military or industrial production units where the whole oper-
ates to greater effect than the sum of the constituent parts). In
Foucault's terms:

> 'Discipline' may be identified neither with an institution nor
> with an apparatus; it is a type of power, a modality for its
> exercise, comprising a whole set of instruments, techniques,
> procedures, levels of application, targets; it is a 'physics'
> or an anatomy of power, a technology. And it may be taken
> over either by 'specialized' institutions (the penitentiaries
> ...) or by institutions that use it as an essential instrument
> for a particular end (schools ...), or ... by pre-existing
> authorities ... or finally by state apparatuses whose major,
> if not exclusive, function is to assure that discipline reigns
> over society as a whole (the police). (Ibid., pp. 215-16)

The process of diffusion of discipline throughout the social
domain is synonymous with what Foucault has, somewhat ambiguously, described as the formation of a disciplinary society.
In order to clarify this conception of a disciplinary society and
to explore its ambiguities it is necessary to consider a distinction between two senses of discipline. On the one hand there
is the discipline-blockade, 'the enclosed institution, established
on the edges of society, turned inwards towards negative functions' (ibid., p. 209). On the other hand there is that new
political anatomy of detail which is the conception of discipline
as a general formula of domination, an appropriate representation of which is Bentham's 'Panopticon'. Bentham's 'Panopticon'
has been described by Foucault as the architectural configuration of the new mechanism of power, as 'a marvellous machine
which ... produces homogeneous effects of power', which offers
a facility for individualising observation, as well as for the

training or correction of individuals, whilst simultaneously assuring the automatic and disindividualising exercise of that very same power.

The Panopticon constitutes a generalisable model of a mechanism of power. In its 'ideal form' the architectural construction of a field of visibility, in which the observer remains unseen, creates a relationship of power in which those who are subject to observation and conscious of their visibility conspire to produce their own subjection. In addition, such a construction lends itself to experimentation on individuals, to the assessment of different modes of training or treatment, and to the observation of effects. A panoptic mechanism may be deployed in a variety of contexts where a multiplicity of individuals are located (e.g. hospitals, schools, prisons, factories, and workshops), its effect being to make possible an improvement in the quantity, quality, intensity, and efficacy of the exercise of power. The diffusion of 'panopticism' throughout the social body is therefore associated with a general amplification of power which does not curb or limit social forces, but rather produces their enhancement.

Bentham's 'Panopticon' contains both a model of a perfect disciplinary institution (the discipline-blockade) and indirectly a formula for the generalisation of the disciplines throughout the whole social body. The disciplines may therefore be deployed beyond the discipline-blockade in a programme for a generalised surveillance of the whole social body. As Foucault has remarked:

> The movement from one project to the other ... rests on a historical transformation: the gradual extension of the mechanisms throughout the seventeenth and eighteenth centuries, ... the formation of what might be called in general the disciplinary society. (Ibid., p. 209)

THE DISCIPLINARY SOCIETY

Whereas the initial extension of disciplinary institutions was directed towards the neutralisation of problems, the general process of diffusion through which discipline became a general formula of domination was inherently positive and directed towards increasing the utility of individuals. For example, military discipline became less a preventive measure to stop desertion, disobedience, and destruction of property and much more of a mechanism for achieving a unity from the assembled ranks of individual soldiers, enhancing coordination, skill, and ultimately therefore the performance of the whole unit. In the case of the factory or workshop, discipline might have continued to exercise a moral regulation of behaviour, but its importance has increasingly rested with its cultivation of improvements in performance and thereby the productivity and profitability of the enterprise.

Besides fabricating useful individuals, the disciplines also circulated in a dispersed form throughout the social body, providing flexible methods of control through the surveillance of populations. For example, the Christian school not only produced trained and docile children, it in addition constituted a mechanism for the supervision of parents. The manifest function of the school may have been the training of children, but in the performance of this function it extended a form of supervision and surveillance over parents, and gathered necessary information on their morality, material resources, and ways of living. Thus, even where disciplinary procedures were located within quasi-enclosed institutions, it is evident that their effectivity was not confined to the members of such institutions alone. It is when disciplinary mechanisms of power have become diffused throughout the social body, infiltrating and undermining other modalities of power, that reference may be made to the formation of a disciplinary society.

The emergence of a disciplinary society has been situated by Foucault alongside a number of broad historical processes. These are as follows:

(i) demographic-economic
(ii) juridico-political
(iii) scientific

In a manner which bears a resemblance to Durkheim's discussion of social development (the decline of mechanical solidarity and concomitant emergence of organic solidarity, individualism, and the division of labour), Foucault has suggested that the development of disciplinary methods corresponded to a particular demographic-economic historical conjuncture, namely the increase in population in the eighteenth century and the associated 'growth in the apparatus of production'. In brief, the disciplines provided the appropriate techniques for securing and administering the larger and more dense population units and for improving the efficiency and profitability of the apparatuses of production (of wealth, health, knowledge, and destruction). Although I do not intend in this context to pursue the question of resemblances between Foucault's analysis of the development of the disciplines and Durkheim's discussion of social development, it is worth noting, if only as an additional clarification of the conception of disciplinary power, that the reality defined by Durkheim as the subject matter of sociology, namely the social, is synonymous for Foucault with the network of disciplinary power. It is here, in relation to the operation of this specific technology of power, that we may locate the emergence of the subject matter of the human sciences, that we may uncover their historical conditions of possibility.

The terms in which Foucault has described the development of disciplinary methods and their correspondence with a particular historical conjuncture invite another comparison, this time with

Marxist analysis. Whereas a conception of economic determination in the final instance might be regarded as the very cornerstone of a historical materialist analysis, in Foucault's work
events are analysed according to the multiple processes by
which they are constituted. Therefore, references to the importance of economic production and of techniques for the accumulation of capital in the historical process of formation of our
society are qualified by comparable references to events of
equivalent significance, in particular the development and diffusion of methods for administering populations. As Foucault
has commented:

> If the economic take-off of the West began with the techni-
> ques that made possible the accumulation of capital, it might
> perhaps be said that the methods for administering the
> accumulation of men made possible a political take-off.... In
> fact the two processes - the accumulation of men and the
> accumulation of capital - cannot be separated; it would not
> have been possible to solve the problem of the accumulation
> of men without the growth of an apparatus of production
> capable of both sustaining them and using them; conversely,
> the techniques that made the cumulative multiplicity of men
> useful accelerated the accumulation of capital. (1977b,
> pp. 220-1)

At a more general level what is at issue is a question of the
relationship between power and mode of production. The implication in Foucault's work is that relations of power are not
secondary or subordinate to the mode of production and therefore should not be conceptualised as effecting simply a maintenance or reproduction of the latter; rather power should be
conceptualised as constitutive of the mode of production. An
example might make this clearer.

In Foucault's view the existence of labour-power, a prerequisite for the capitalist mode of production, may not simply be
assumed to be synonymous with the human condition; rather it
has to be produced or fabricated. An explanation of labour-
power cannot be derived either from references to the family
as the site of biological reproduction and source of restoration
or replenishment of spent labour-power, or from references
to the social conditions which facilitated the availability of
formally free labourers, for example the enclosure movement,
the shift of population from the land to towns and cities. To
account for the existence of labour-power it is necessary to
recognise the specificity of work under the modern factory
system of production and that on which it depends for its possibility, namely discipline. Discipline is a power which infiltrates
the very body and psyche of the individual, which, in this
instance, transforms the life and time of the individual into
labour-power, that property essential to the capitalist mode of
production. To integrate individuals into the apparatus of

production requires that a significant part of their life-time is constituted as labour-time - a time in which labour-power is available to be expended. In other words, human energy, life, must be transformed into a commodity which is continuous and constantly available in the market place. This is achieved through discipline, through particular methods which have made possible a precise control of the operations of the body, the effect of which has been a maximisation of the body as a useful force and a reduction or regulation of the body as a political force.

Although Foucault has made reference to the economic aspect of the historical conjuncture in which a development of disciplinary methods occurred, the focus of his analysis has been upon the methods by which it became possible to ensure a control over the operations of the body and a constant subjection of its forces, on the functioning of the disciplines as techniques for fabricating useful individuals - individuals capable of being inserted into the apparatus of production. The growth of a capitalist economy may have been referred to as a significant feature of the historical conjuncture associated with the formation of the disciplinary society, however discipline, the technology of power linked with the emergence of the human sciences, remains inexplicable in terms of deductions from the economy. An understanding of the event described as the formation of the disciplinary society cannot be generated from an analysis of the mode of production.

The second broad historical process considered to be of significance for the formation of the disciplinary society is juridico-political and concerns the nature of the relationship between the disciplines and the juridical and political structures of society. Foucault has observed that the process by which the bourgeoisie became the politically dominant social class was in fact concealed by the existence of a 'formally egalitarian juridical framework', which in principle guaranteed an egalitarian system of rights. Beneath the juridical structure, and supporting it, was a network of micro-powers, the disciplines, which are non-egalitarian, asymmetrical, and ultimately 'counter-law'. In other words, the disciplines represent the reality of the functioning of power, providing the foundation on which the formal juridical structure is predicated, and yet effectively operate in opposition to the formal egalitarianism of the latter. Thus the disciplines evade and undermine the formal juridical limitations on the exercise of power, whilst simultaneously guaranteeing 'the submission of forces and bodies', which constitutes the necessary foundation of the legal and political structures of modern society.

The final historical process connected with the formation of the disciplinary society has been described by Foucault as 'scientific'. Briefly it concerns the emergence in the eighteenth century of a combination and generalisation of disciplinary techniques, such that an inter-relationship emerged between

the exercise of power and the formation of knowledge. The
disciplines transformed the institutions in which they functioned into apparatuses within which methods for the formation
and accumulation of knowledge began to be employed as instruments of domination and increases in power began to produce
an addition to knowledge.

The conception of a disciplinary society might seem to be
derived from the very form of global or systematising theory
to which genealogical analysis and research stands opposed –
a possible implication of the term being that modern societies
have become disciplined societies, orderly and programmed
realities which allow little or no opposition or resistance. However, an interpretation of the conception of the disciplinary
society as a 'disciplined' society is remiss for three reasons.

To begin with, the process of diffusion of the disciplines
throughout society, the emergence of a generalised network of
surveillance, constitutes a general formula of domination, the
emphasis being upon panopticism, generalised surveillance,
as a formula, rather than as a completely installed mechanism
functioning at an optimum level to produce a programmed society.
Foucault's conception of the disciplinary society does indeed
refer to the extension of disciplinary mechanisms, to the diffusion of a formula beyond the 'discipline-blockade', but it
does not signify the realisation of a programme for a disciplined
and ordered society. Second, although Foucault has provided
relatively little discussion or comment on resistances or struggles against and around the exercise of power, it is quite clear
that such practices are considered to be an inherent feature of
social life and of relations of power in particular. This serves
to further undermine interpretations which conflate the conception of the disciplinary society with that of a disciplined society.
Finally, implicit in the interpretation of the disciplinary society
as equivalent to a disciplined society is a conception of a close
correspondence between rationalities and the functioning of
institutions, the implication being that a disciplinary rationality
may materialise or be realised in the form of a disciplined society.
Such a conception is the very antithesis of the position outlined by Foucault, which is that programmes never work out as
planned – in other words, that the normal relationship between
programmes and practices is one of non-correspondence.

DISCOURSES, PRACTICES, AND EFFECTS

Whereas within the discourses of the human sciences, and in
particular in the field of policy studies, there is a conception
of the social world as a potentially rationalisable order, as a
reality which might be rendered orderly through the implementation of 'social engineering' techniques of intervention derived
from instrumental-rational analyses, in the work of Foucault
the implied relationship between discourses, practices, and

effects is of a very different order. What is at issue here is
the nature of the interplay between forms of rationality and
specific institutional practices, in particular the fact that programmes or rational schemas offering a formula for the reorgan-
isation of institutions and for the regulation of human multiplicities have not been realised in social practices - in short,
that there has been an evident lack of correspondence between
programmes, practices, and effects.

A conception of a possible correspondence between discursive
formulations, social and institutional practices, and effects - a
conception which implies the possibility of 'successful' social
policies, policies producing intended effects, effects as programmed - has been part of the foundation of the human
sciences. As I have indicated, Foucault's analyses exemplify
the converse position, namely that social institutions and human
behaviour are perpetually more complex than any programmatic
formulation, with the result that there is always a lack of
correspondence. The implication of Foucault's position is not
that programmes are really little more than models, fictions, or
imaginary constructions with virtually no relevance to the real
world. A lack of correspondence does not signify the absence
of a relationship between programmes, practices and effects;
rather it demonstrates the complexity of the social world, and
implies, first, that effects are other than explicitly programmed,
and second, that the relationship of non-correspondence, or,
to put it more positively, the actual, if unintended effects of
programmes, should be examined. Foucault's analysis of the
'failure' of the prison constitutes one illustration of the complexity of this relationship of non-correspondence (cf. Smart,
1983).

Within the human sciences non-correspondence has frequently
been conceptualised in terms of the unintended consequences of
human action (cf. Ryan, 1970); indeed, the very field of study
of the human sciences might be described as the relationship
between intentions, actions, and consequences. The form in
which this issue has increasingly been explored within sociology
is in terms of an analysis of the relationship between structure
and agency (cf. Giddens, 1979; Smart, 1982). However, the most
common reference point has remained the work of Weber, in
particular his formulation of the unintended consequences of the
asceticism of Calvinism, namely the creation of a spirit conducive to the development of a specific mode of economic activity,
modern capitalism (cf. Weber, 1976). I will give consideration to
the question of similarities and differences between the respective analyses of Weber and Foucault in the next chapter.

ON SOCIAL REGULATION, GOVERNMENT AND THE STATE

I have already noted that the disciplines constitute merely one
of the dimensions along which a power over life has been

exercised; another, at least equally significant dimension has
been the management or regulation of the species 'body', or
population. The difference between the two respective dimensions is one of scale; it represents a distinction between what
might be termed 'microscopic' techniques, the object of which
is a disciplining of individuals, of the individual body, and
'macroscopic' techniques, which are directed towards a regulation of population. It is to the latter, to the emergence of
techniques for the regulation of population, to the process by
which the administration or regulation of population became a
matter of, and for, an art of government, that I will now turn
my attention.

The problematic of government has been identified by Foucault as a phenomenon which surfaced in the sixteenth century
in the form of a series of discourses and questions about self-
government and codes of conduct: 'the government of souls
and lives'; the government of children; and in addition the
government of the state. At the centre of the problematic of
government there was a debate between two positions. In one,
government was conceptualised as equivalent to the form of
rule exercised by a sovereign over a principality, a corollary
of which was that the power of the sovereign was to be distinguished from other forms of power. In the second, practices
of government were identified as variable in form, location, and
for that matter agency, but underlying each of the respective
forms there was a common denominator, a specific art of government. The importance of the latter, of an art of government,
was that it represented an attempt at provision of a rationality
for government, and thereby for the state, that was independent of any conception of the interests of a sovereign ruler.
This alternative and oppositional rationality was articulated in
terms of 'economy', specifically in terms of an analogy between
a wise government of the family and government of the state.

At the centre of Foucault's discussion of the problematic of
government, and in a manner comparable with his analysis of
changes in the mode and object of punishment, there is a cate-
gorical distinction between one form of the exercise of power
sovereignty - which has as its object the preservation of a
principality or territory, and a submission of the people to the
authority of the law by which sovereign rule is preserved, or
rather, with which it it synonymous - and another form,
government, for which the target is 'the complex unit constituted by men and things', and the object is to manage, to
facilitate an optimal realisation of the ends appropriate to, and
convenient for, each of the respective entities subject to
government. Whereas with sovereignty the end is the very
preservation of sovereignty itself, the principal mechanism being the authority of law, in the case of government the focus
of concern is the relationship between people and things; human
relationships; wealth and resources; ways of living; and the
contingencies to which the human condition is exposed (e.g.

accidents, epidemics, famines, etc.), with government of the
state ultimately being likened to 'a form of surveillance, of
control which is as watchful as that of the head of a family over
his household and his goods' (Foucault, 1979b, p. 10).

The catalyst for the development of the problematic of government beyond the 'models' of sovereignty and the family was the
emergence of the phenomenon of population. With the constitution of the phenomenon of population as an object of knowledge
the problematic of government could be formulated independently
of both the juridical framework of sovereignty and the model of
the family. The phenomenon of population emerged as an object
of government with the demographic expansion of the eighteenth
century. Statistical forms of representation revealed that population had its own regularities (e.g. birth and death rates,
characteristic ailments, etc.) and that these were irreducible
to the level of the family. Such representations indicated that
population is a higher-order phenomenon of which the family is
one dimension, a consequence of which was a displacement of
the family as the model of government; instead the family became, as Donzelot (1980) has documented, a privileged instrument for the regulation or management of population. Thus the
aim or end of government, a complex new form of power, became
the welfare of the population, the administration of measures to
improve health and wealth.

A few qualificatory comments on the issue of the historical
emergence of specific forms of power-knowledge relations might
obviate a possible misunderstanding. There is no conception of
an evolutionary, or linear, historical succession of forms of the
exercise of power in Foucault's work. Sovereignty does not
cease to exist, and in turn discipline does not decline with the
advent of apparatuses of government and 'insurantial technologies'. We are not, in other words, presented with an evolutionary schema of sovereignty-discipline-government; rather
the latter are conceptualised in terms of a triangular relationship targeted on population. The concept of sovereignty remains
relevant to the question of the form of the legitimacy of the
state deploying techniques of government, for it addresses the
legal foundation of the state, and discipline continues to manifest itself at the level of the management of population in its
details, in its individualities. As Foucault has concluded:

> The notion of a government of population renders all the
> more acute the problem of the foundation of sovereignty ...
> and all the more acute equally the necessity for the devel-
> opment of disciplines. (1979b, p. 19)

Nevertheless, the respective dimensions of the triangular relationship between sovereignty-discipline-government are not
equivalent. Foucault has commented that the tendency within the
West has been for government to achieve a pre-eminence over
both sovereignty and discipline; that is to say, for control to

be exercised increasingly through apparatuses of security and insurance, via 'insurantial technologies' (cf. Donzelot, 1979).

THE STATE AND 'THE SOCIAL'

The social is an enigmatic and worrying figure of which no-one wants to take stock for fear of losing one's way or one's Lenin. (Donzelot, 1979, p. 85)

In his analyses of forms of the exercise of power Foucault has deliberately decentred the question of the state. I want to comment briefly on the direct implications of the work of Foucault, Pasquino, and Donzelot for our understanding of the state and its place in the order of things.

Within contemporary political theory and analysis the issue of the state has assumed an enormous significance. In the works of the 'new philosophers' the centralised state constitutes the dreadful promise and logic of totalitarian tendencies within Marxism (cf. Lévy, 1979). In the case of Marxism the state, albeit conceptualised as servicing or guaranteeing the development of productive forces and the reproduction of relations of production, has been depicted as the privileged site of the exercise of power which needs must be captured or infiltrated if a programme of radical social transformation is to have any chance of success. In contrast to both of these positions Foucault, Pasquino and Donzelot have suspended assumptions concerning the unity, functionality, and importance of the state.

In the case of Foucault a suspension of assumptions concerning the state has manifested itself in the form of an examination of the emergence of the tactics and techniques of government, of the administration or regulation of population. Rather than assuming state domination of society and then proceeding to an analysis of the respective state apparatuses, modes of operation, and forms of representation of ruling-class interests, Foucault has speculated that the state may only be comprehended through an analysis of the tactics and techniques of government by which its effects are produced. A comparable formulation is to be found in the work of Pasquino (1978). Pasquino has argued that genealogies of history which privilege capital are now bankrupt, principally as a consequence of their neglect of technologies of power and concomitant fixation on 'the State as an apparatus or instance separate from the social body'. To proceed further we need to take a different tack: consideration has to be given to the processes by which the social body was constituted as an object of knowledge and as a target for the exercise of power. Pasquino has proposed that we might begin by examining one of the elements identified by Foucault as forming the basis of 'the governmentalisation of the State', namely police.

The concept of police has not always referred to the maintenance of a legal order or to a surveillance of the 'dangerous classes'. In the eighteenth century its reference was to the promotion of the public good, to the public interest conceived in the broadest of senses and encompassing a wide range of objects. The science of police, as Pasquino has noted, consti- tuted 'a great labour of formation ... of the social body, or rather a labour whose principal result is what today we call society or the social body and what the eighteenth century called the good order of population' (ibid., p. 47).

The emergence of police regulations signifies the beginning of the exercise of a power of administration over the social body – an exercise of power which had two particular aims, the attain- ment of information and the cultivation of happiness, and which simultaneously constituted population as an object of knowledge and a target for power. It is in the practices and knowledges of 'police, assistance ... medicalisation ... the prison, sexuality, psychiatry' (ibid., p. 52) that we encounter the orderly network of 'the social', the locus or field of relations of power. From this Pasquino and Donzelot, like Foucault, have concluded that to comprehend the exercise of power, to develop an analysis of the positivity of power, requires at the very least a suspension, if not an abandonment, of the conception of the state as the locus or prime operator of power.

An analysis of 'the social' as an object of particular power- knowledge relations should be distinguished from the more con- ventional analyses of society to be found in the human sciences. Within the latter 'society' has constituted an ahistorical conception of the necessary and universal form of human existence. In contrast the concept of 'the social' denotes a particular historical event, namely the emergence of a network or relay of institutions and functions through which a productive or positive power is exercised over populations. As Donzelot has noted, there is a significant difference between the two terms:

'the social' is not society understood as the set of material and moral conditions that characterize a form of consolida- tion. It would appear to be rather the set of means which allow social life to escape material pressures and politico- moral uncertainties; the entire range of methods which make the members of society relatively safe from the effects of economic fluctuations by providing a certain security. (1980, p. xxvi)

The concept of 'the social', as distinct from that of society, signifies a specific level or sector which is synonymous with the emergence and development of a series of technologies of power. The emergence of 'the social', and the associated mea- sures and mechanisms directed towards such dimensions of population as fertility, age, health, economic activity, welfare, and education, not only represents a major development or shift in the form of the exercise of power, but in addition it has

produced significant changes in the nature of social relationships, and has since the mid-nineteenth century effected a
particular form of cohesion or solidarity within society.

It is at the political level that the various measures and technologies of power associated with the rise of 'the social' have
had their most critical impact, the insertion of a 'principle of
cohesion' in the very fabric of society being synonymous with
a transformation of the nature of social divisions, struggles,
and conflicts. One important possible consequence of this
development, outlined by Donzelot, is that the conventional
dichotomies and concepts which have structured orthodox radical and critical analyses have largely become obsolete, for the
introduction of social measures (e.g. allowances and benefits
to provide compensation for unemployment, illness, and old
age; and the practices of assistance and reform associated with
social work) has precipitated a socialisation of politics, a sub-
sumption of 'the political into the social'. The implication being
that particular conditions, which in the nineteenth century were
a source of political controversy, have been transformed in
significant respects.

For example, Donzelot has argued that both the question of
unemployment and that of the relation between employers/
management and workers have been transformed by the advent
of insurantial technologies. In the case of unemployment, provision has been made for an allowance, a 'wage', in order to
provide a minimal degree of security for individuals and families,
and this has had the effect of engendering a shift 'from a situation in which man defined himself as worker confronting capital
to a situation in which he is an employee of society (whether
he is working or not)' (1979, p. 81). In respect of relations
between employers and workers the introduction of legislation
on safety, hygiene, collective bargaining, and work contracts
has effected a comparable 'socialisation of the relation of employment'. Such measures, such exercises of power, have provided
sites around which a knowledge has formed, an 'industrial
knowledge', and this has, in turn, provided a foundation for
the development of political decision-making towards an increasingly close embrace of technocratic formulae of social management.

Given that politics has been reduced to a technical question
of social management, we may conclude that not only has the
antagonistic polarity of political discourses, exemplified by
'the theory-programmes of the nineteenth century', become
something of an anachronism, but furthermore, to continue to
conceptualise and to analyse politics and power in terms derived
from traditional political culture will ensure a repetition of the
very omissions and weaknesses which have been associated
with the limitations of radical political culture. Hence the different orientation revealed in the work of Foucault, Pasquino,
and Donzelot, notably a suspension of assumptions concerning
the state, and a compensatory focus on the emergence of the

social and associated technologies of power.

The issue of the state has received little direct attention in Foucault's major studies, but its importance has belatedly been explicitly acknowledged in the form of a statement that 'power relations have come more and more under state control ... have been progressively governmentalised, that is to say, elaborated, rationalised and centralised in the form of or under the auspices of, state institutions' (cf. 1982, p. 224). Although this statement does not signify a change in Foucault's conception of the analysis of power relations – indeed, the view that such relations are not derived from the political structure of the state but are 'rooted deep in the social nexus' is simultaneously reaffirmed – it nevertheless does imply a degree of accommodation to the criticism that there had formerly been a neglect of the state (cf. Poulantzas, 1978, pp. 44, 77).

The distinctiveness of the modern state in Foucault's view lies in its utilisation of individualising techniques of power; however, it is not the political structure of the state which has constituted the immediate object of analysis but the emergence and development of individualising techniques of power with which the state has become linked. In brief, the question of the institutional form of the state has been de-centred in preference for an analysis of the particular individualising techniques of power and cultural modes of objectification to which human beings in modern societies have become increasingly subject. In other words, whereas within Marxist analysis the question of the state has increasingly occupied a central position, in Foucault's work the emphasis has been on the analysis of power relations within society, relations which 'cannot be reduced to the study of a series of institutions' (cf. 1982, p. 224). Nevertheless, in the final instance Foucault's work does bear on the question of the state in so far as it provides an analysis of those individualising techniques of power which have in various forms become integrated within or linked to the institutions of the modern state.

6 CRITICAL ANALYSES OF RATIONALITY

I have described the common denominator in Foucault's several studies as a critical concern with the question of the relationship between forms of rationality and forms of power. The identification of such a common theme in Foucault's work invites a comparison with two other types of analysis which have presented criticisms of the effects of particular forms of rationality, namely those to be found in the work of Max Weber and in the work of the critical theorists of the Frankfurt School. Comparison will be restricted to an exploration of what might seem to be parallel themes and conceptual similarities between the work of Foucault and that of Weber and the Frankfurt School respectively.

WEBER

There are five particular issues which constitute the basis of my comparison of the work of Max Weber with that of Foucault:

(i) rationality
(ii) historical analysis
(iii) power and domination
(iv) discipline
(v) the paradox of consequences

In Weber's work one persistent and central theme is that the world in which we live, and will continue to live in the future, is characterised by and subject to a process of increasing rationalisation. By this Weber meant a process of scientific specialisation and technical differentiation associated with Western culture, the objective of which has been the pursuit of a mastery over the social and physical environment. The process of rationalisation, through a steady dispersal and diffusion of methods of calculation and control, has effected a gradual disenchantment of the world. However, such a process should not be considered equivalent to, or for that matter be interpreted as, a sign of progress. The development within Western culture of a propensity towards the exercise of a control or mastery over nature and culture was not regarded by Weber as indicative of an advance in our understanding of life. Rather, the implication is that such a development signified, not only a lack of understanding of the limits of our ability to exercise a control over nature and culture, in other words a simultaneous advance of 'error' along with that of rationality, but also a lack of awareness of the effect of attempts to extend a control over life. For Weber the process of increasing rational-isation was paradoxically associated both with an increase in the intensity of irrationality and with a further exacerbation of the alienation of the human condition.

The process of rationalisation does not then represent the progress of reason, neither does it signify an increase in aware-ness or enlightenment. Rationalisation bears on the social and physical environment and is directed towards a regulation, control, and ultimate mastery of the same. Its focus has been the production of 'efficient' forms of social organisation, rather than a construction of the preconditions necessary for individual or collective moral progress. Rationalisation has precipitated discontent and disenchantment in and with the present as it has constantly held out the promise of a better future, a state which has inevitably continually receded with the attainment of each new advance in the process of rationalisation. Hence Weber's fear, articulated in his critical observations on the future of Soviet socialism in particular, that the process of rationalisation would exacerbate rather than alleviate the difficulties of the human condition.

The process of rationalisation to which Weber has referred is one of constant refinement and development of the means by which specific effects or goals, themselves not subject to rational inquiry or investigation, might be realised. As such, rationality does not constitute a basis on which conflicts arising from competing evaluations might be resolved. To put it more simply, we may note that Weber, following Nietzsche, has argued that scientific rationality, instrumental reason, is un-able to provide grounds for arbitration between antagonistic values or conflicting goals. As Weber has commented:

> After Nietzsche's devastating criticism of the 'last men' who 'invented happiness', I may leave aside altogether the naive optimism in which science - that is, the technique of master-ing life which rests upon science - has been celebrated as the way to happiness. (1970, p. 143)

The realm of values, of justice, freedom, beauty, and goodness, lies beyond the perimeter of instrumental reason. Furthermore, just as rationality is unable to provide grounds or criteria for qualitative judgments, for differentiating between values, so in addition it is unable to anticipate the future. As the events it seeks to explain and to order are complex, being the product of a multiplicity of factors or preconditions, a high degree of indeterminacy is always present. Here we encounter the place of chance or accident in history, a familiar theme in Nietzsche's work and one indirectly taken up by Weber and Foucault.

For Weber rationalisation seems to have assumed the form of

an all-encompassing historical process, its impact being evident
within economic enterprises, in the bureaucratic administration
of the state, and in a general intellectualisation or disenchantment of the world. In so far as the focus of Weber's analysis
has been on rationalisation as a global process, as a historical
process which increasingly shapes all manner of social relationships and actions, then there is a significant difference from
Foucault's work, the object of the latter being forms of rationality or rationalities examined 'in several fields each of them
grounded in a fundamental experience' (Foucault, 1981b, p. 226)
rather than rationality conceived as a global process or as an
anthropological invariant. A second difference between the two
types of analysis arises from the above.
   Weber's account of the effect of a progressive rationalisation
of the world conveys a sense of both resignation and despair
about the human condition and its prospects. Our fate is to be
confined within an 'iron cage' of instrumental reason and to be
subjected to bureaucratic forms of domination; it is to be one of
increasing alienation, from which it is implied there will be no
escape. Even socialism, the source of hope and reference for
so many people interested in a positive transformation and
improvement of the human condition, would in Weber's view
produce merely a higher degree of rigid bureaucratic administration and control. The process of rationalisation connected
with the capitalist mode of production is not therefore destined
to disappear with the advent of socialism. On the contrary,
Weber argued that the restoration and maintenance of production which would be necessary in a socialist system would
require a greater degree of work-discipline, and that to achieve
this an even more rigorous form of bureaucratic domination
would be required, one effect of which would be an increase
in the degree of general domination exercised over individuals,
and another a further erosion of 'non-rational' human values.
Perhaps we should note in passing that Weber reached these
conclusions without the benefits of hindsight available to the
'new philosophers'.
   Although Foucault's analyses of the relationship between forms
of rationality, forms of power and their effects, and his general
antipathy towards actually existing socialism, evident in the
series of comments on the 'Gulag question', point to the possibility of a considerable degree of common ground with the
work of Weber, in fact commonality is largely confined to a
critical orientation to the effects of rationalisation, and even on
this score differences remain.
   To begin with, the conception of rationality employed by
Foucault does not refer to a constant global historical process;
rather the focus, as I have already observed, is on forms of
rationality, on rationalities. In consequence, where a conception
of rationality has been employed, it takes on an instrumental
and relative meaning. For example, as Foucault has commented:

The ceremony of public torture isn't in itself more irrational than imprisonment in a cell; but it's irrational in terms of a type of penal practice which involves new ways of envisaging the effects to be produced by the penalty imposed, new ways of calculating its utility, justifying it, graduating it, etc. (1981a, p. 8)

Thus there is no absolute form of rationality against which specific forms might be compared or evaluated; rather it is a matter, for Foucault, of investigating the rationalities inscribed within different social practices, of determining how a particular 'regime of rationality' simultaneously constitutes rules and procedures for doing things (e.g. training individuals) and produces 'true' discourses which legitimate these activities, by providing them with reasons and principles.

Further, whereas Weber presents the process of rationalisation and disenchantment of the world as virtually irreversible, save for the remote prospect of a regeneration of charisma, Foucault has consistently discussed the exercise of power and its rationalities in terms of the perpetual presence of resistance. At no point in Foucault's work does a conceptualisation of forms of rationality and of the exercise of power assume the monolithic dimensions of the process of rationalisation described by Weber. Foucault has quite deliberately avoided a conceptualisation of the problem in terms of the rationalisation of society or culture as a whole, for to proceed in such a manner would be to assume the existence of a single, uniform, and integrated process affecting all forms of human existence and experience. Hence the conception of forms of rationality and the investigation of power-knowledge relations in several fields of human experience.

Although the problematic of rationalisation has been conceptualised by Foucault in terms of a plurality of 'events', rather than as one homogeneous process, the question of other similarities with Weber's work remains. For example, it has been suggested that it is possible to detect the presence of something like a Weberian 'ideal type' category of historical interpretation and analysis in Foucault's work. It is not difficult to understand how such a misinterpretation might arise; however, before investigating this issue further, a brief consideration of the Weberian conception of an 'ideal type' may prove helpful.

In Weber's view the human sciences were necessarily interpretive, selective, and less rigorous than their natural science counterparts - hence the 'ideal type' construction, its purpose being to improve the rigour and precision of analysis in the human sciences. If it is accepted that there is likely to be a variation in the content of ideas from one historical period to another, that the significance or meaning of a particular social practice is likely to vary between cultures and historical periods, then a requirement exists for the appropriate conceptual means to study social phenomena in all their uniqueness or singularity.

For Weber the solution to this particular problem lay in the construction of the ideal type. The ideal type is an analytical construct: it does not represent an empirical instance or reality, and it is not ideal in an ethical sense. It constitutes a unity of the characteristics which are deemed to be distinctive to the particular phenomenon under investigation and it displays a degree of one-sidedness in the sense that it presents a conception of the phenomenon which is partial, where the distinctive characteristics and features are accentuated, and where an emphasis is placed upon the logical (possible) form, rather than upon an existing real form which has emerged from the multiplicity of fluctuating processes of which reality is composed. However, although the ideal type does not represent a conception of an existing phenomenon we should be careful not to conclude that its reference might be to the 'inner' reality or 'true' nature of phenomena. The ideal type serves as a tool for investigation and inquiry for Weber: its purpose is to enable us to derive a better understanding of reality, not to construct a criticism of reality in the light of a potential which remains unrealised.

Foucault has categorically denied a resemblance between his historical analyses of forms of rationality and power and Weber's 'ideal type' analysis. The argument hinges upon a distinction between Weber's concept of the ideal type and Foucault's references to rational schemas or programmes which are not realised in practice. As I have noted, the ideal type is a tool constructed by the researcher-historian to facilitate explanation and understanding of events; it is not, as Foucault has implied, a device which allows the historian 'to recapture an "essence"'. However, although Foucault seems to misunderstand Weber's conception of the ideal type, I believe that there nevertheless remains a fundamental difference between the two modes of analysis.

The crux of the matter concerns Foucault's account of the discrepancy between discourses - for example on punishment and the prison, or on the organisation of the domain of sexuality - and the actual functioning of institutions, which it is evident do not embody a fulfilment of the appropriate rational schemas. The danger here is that the former, the rationalities of punishment, the prison or whatever, may be interpreted as equivalent to ideal types in so far as they are not realised, or to be more precise, in so far as they have no direct and/or complete institutional form. This would be a mistake, for Foucault treats discourses, practices, and effects as three distinctive orders of event. The discourses to which Foucault has referred, the rational schemas of the prison, etc., constitute programmes for the organisation of institutions, and for the regulation of behaviour. Such programmes, in their turn, are derived from other, more general forms of rationality, for example, in the case of penal imprisonment and the Panopticon the appropriate reference would be to the 'disciplines', to a whole technology

of the human body, to surveillance and individualisation. The
point is that the discrepancy between programmes and the functioning of institutions is not synonymous with the distance
between ideal typifications and the empirical reality of phenomena. As Foucault has stated:

> programmes don't take effect in the institutions in an inte-
> gral manner; they are simplified, or some are chosen and
> not others; and things never work out as planned ... this
> difference is not one between the purity of the ideal and
> the disorderly impurity of the real. (1981a, p. 10)

It is not that institutions and social practices are the reality,
and rationalities and programmes merely versions of an ideal
type: on the contrary, rationalities, programmes and technologies are all just as much realities as institutions and social
practices; indeed, such programmes constitute 'fragments of
reality', they induce effects, and it is with these, the unpro-
grammed or unanticipated effects or consequences, that Foucault
has been concerned.

As I have observed, the existence of a relationship of non-
correspondence between programmes, practices, and effects is
of positive interest to Foucault. Evidence of the 'failure' of
social policy has not precipitated a definition of the relationship
of non-correspondence as a problem requiring a solution; rather
it has been conceptualised as a normal feature worthy of serious
investigation. However, although the intended or planned
effects formulated or anticipated within a programme may not
be fulfilled, programmes nevertheless do induce real effects,
they do have an impact on social relations and practices. Perhaps the most obvious example of this position in Foucault's
work is to be found in the discussion of punishment and the
prison to which I have already made reference. In discussing
changes in punishment Foucault has made reference to the
distance between Bentham's disciplinary programme, embodied
in the form of the Panopticon and its operation, and the reality
of penal incarceration, which although modelled on a 'panoptic'
schema and utilising associated disciplinary technologies of
power, never functioned in accordance with Bentham's machine,
and ultimately induced effects which were other than those programmed, namely the production of an enclosed illegality,
delinquency, rather than an elimination or reduction of crime.

Comparison with Weber on this issue effectively underlines
the differences between the two modes of analysis. Foucault
does not construct artificial rationalities to facilitate analysis of
social action and process; rather, existing historical rationalities,
and their complex relationships with social practices and effects,
are the immediate object of analysis.

It might seem that another way of proceeding with a comparison of the work of Weber and that of Foucault would be to
explore their respective conceptions of power. However, such

a comparison tends to underline the essential difference between
the two, for whereas Foucault's analyses construct and employ
a conception of power as positive, productive, and relational,
Weber's work reveals the presence of a juridico-discursive
conception of power. In Weber's work we find power conceptualised in terms of the institutions and mechanisms which produce
subordination, in particular those which are crystallised or
embodied in the form of the state (cf. the essay 'Politics as a
Vocation' in Weber, 1970); as a property, as something that is
'acquired, seized, or shared' (cf. Weber, 1970, pp. 159-232);
and then again in terms of the intentionality of an actor or
agent, where power is 'the probability that one actor within a
social relationship will be in a position to carry out his own
will despite resistance' (Weber, 1966, p. 152). On each count,
as I hope will be clear from my earlier discussion, Foucault's
conception of power manifests a difference; that is to say,
power is not conceptualised in terms of the state, or the intentionality of actors or agents, as a property or a possession,
or finally as purely repressive or prohibitive.

ON DISCIPLINE AND THE ROUTINISATION OF CHARISMA

If we turn to Weber's more precise conception of a 'special
case of power', namely domination, and to the modes of legitimation of domination in particular, then it is possible to recognise another, possibly more productive point of comparison
with the work of Foucault.
   In the course of his discussion of the legitimation of domination Weber has differentiated between three rationales for
obedience, what have come to be known as three types of
authority: namely a bureaucratic or legal-rational authority,
which is associated with the advance of rationalism, and two
others, a patriarchal or traditional authority and a charismatic
authority. In Weber's view both traditional and charismatic
authority have been steadily eroded, even destroyed, by the
steady proliferation of legal-rational authority. However, in all
other respects charismatic authority should be differentiated
from traditional authority, and for that matter from legal-
rational authority, for the latter have in common an important
quality, namely a degree of permanence; they are, in Weber's
terms, 'both institutions of daily routine ... rooted in the
provisioning of recurrent and normal needs of the workaday
life' (1970, p. 245). In contrast charismatic authority refers
to the non-routine, to disruptions of everyday routine, to a
legitimation of domination grounded in the extraordinary and
personal qualities of an individual leader.
   The concept of charisma has a special place and function
within Weber's work. In so far as Weber's analyses of history
rotate around a general conception of a continuous process of
rationalisation and its effects, the conception of charisma has

provided the requisite means for 'thinking' discontinuities, for
identifying those moments of crisis when everyday routines are
disrupted or destroyed. The concept of charisma has allowed
Weber to accommodate interruptions in the continuous historical
process of rationalisation, to qualify the social determinism
inherent in a conception of the inexorable extension of the
process of rationalisation. However, it has constituted only a
minor qualification, for in the final instance Weber seems to
have reached the pessimistic conclusion that the ultimate fate
of charisma will be one of routinisation into a legal-rational
form. Nevertheless, the concept of charisma retains a meta-
physical value in Weber's work; it constitutes the sole locus of
a possible, if temporary, freedom for the individual from processes of social determination in general, and rationalisation
in particular.

Weber has argued that behind the decline of charisma there
lies the 'diminishing importance of individual action' and that
the most significant predisposing factor in this process is
'rational discipline'. Although the concept of discipline does not
directly signify a form of power, its reference is to a mode of
social action involving unswerving obedience which may be
appropriated or employed in the service of power (cf. Weber,
1968, p. 1149). Furthermore, Weber's subsequent discussion
of discipline bears a close resemblance to that disciplinary
technology of power conceptualised by Foucault. For example,
Weber has commented that discipline is rational, methodic,
and impersonal, that it is detailed, and involves a rational
calculation of physical and psychic factors. In addition, the
significant influence of the military institution and the structure
of warfare on the emergence and development of rational discipline has been emphasised, again in a manner comparable to
Foucault's discussion of the signs of the emergence in the
eighteenth century of the exercise of disciplinary methods
within armies, methods which produced 'subjected and prac-
tised bodies, "docile bodies"' (1977b, p. 138). Finally, Weber
has argued that the more lasting and significant effects of
discipline are to be found within the social and political order,
in 'the structure of the State, the economy, and possibly the
family' (1968, p. 1153), a conclusion which has, to some extent,
received an implicit endorsement in the respective analyses of
social technologies of power and their effects conducted by
Foucault, Pasquino, and Donzelot.

According to Weber military discipline was the origin of all
discipline: in particular it constituted the ideal model for large-
scale economic organisations like the modern capitalist factory.
In discussing the impact of rational-discipline at work Weber
has observed:

The psycho-physical apparatus of man is completely adjusted
to the demands of the outer world, the tools, the machines -
in short, it is functionalized, and the individual is shorn of

his natural rhythm as determined by his organism; in line with the demands of the work procedure, he is attuned to a new rhythm through the functional specialization of muscles and through the creation of an optimal economy of physical effort. (Ibid., p. 1156)

The process described by Weber, of the production of docile and useful bodies - what might in this particular instance be termed the disciplinary fabrication of labour-power - constitutes a central feature of the formation of the disciplinary society analysed by Foucault. Indeed, we might regard Foucault's analysis of disciplinary technologies of power as a more precise and detailed investigation, in one particular field (e.g. penal incarceration and its effects), of the general process to which Weber has referred.

However, despite similarities, an important difference remains, namely that one implication of Weber's comments on the waning of charisma, as a consequence of the emergence and development of rational discipline, is that it is an irresistible process, that there is no resistance to discipline. In contrast, whilst analysing the emergence of a new political economy of the body and associated disciplinary technologies of power, Foucault has emphasised the perpetual presence of forms of resistance and struggle and has concluded that social and historical processes are therefore necessarily subject to a high degree of indeterminacy. Thus, whereas Weber seems to have assumed an unceasing extension of rationalisation, the implication being that the fate of charisma and the human condition is already determined, Foucault has sought to investigate and to challenge the rationalities in use in particular fields, to provide a critical analysis of their emergence and their effects, the implication being that the rationalisation of relations of power may be undermined, that liberation remains a possibility, but only by 'attacking ... political rationality's very roots' (1981b, p. 254).

Finally, a brief comment on another possible comparison, to which I have already alluded, namely between the conception of the unintended consequences or effects of human action and the conception of a relationship of non-correspondence between programmes, practices, and effects in the works of Weber and Foucault respectively.

Weber emphasised the indeterminacy surrounding social action; that is to say, the results of human action were likely not to be in accord with the intentions of the participants, the subjects of action. At one level Weber's work attempts to explain how particular ways of conceiving the world may have effects other than those intended or anticipated. The whole process of rationalisation, and the concomitant attempt to extend a form of control over the social and physical environment, represents one example, the evident effect being not only the possible achievement of a greater degree of security for the human condition, but in addition the emergence of other, more explicitly

negative consequences, such as an increase in depersonalisation
and oppressive routine, and a further erosion or curtailment of
personal freedom. Foucault's work on the relationship of non-
correspondence between programmes, practices, and effects
represents a 'further means of exploring the positive significance' of the paradox of unintended consequences described
by Weber (cf. Gordon, 1979, pp. 36-7).

By way of a summary we may note that there are particular
parallel themes and comparable formulations in the respective
works of Weber and Foucault, and that in addition to the issues
discussed above there are a range of other matters on which a
degree of common ground might be shown to exist: for example,
the influence on the formation of their thought of the respective
works of Marx and Nietzsche; the existence of a comparable
critical orientation and general scepticism towards socialism,
and its effect on social life and the human condition; and the
presence of a common criticism of the idea that any one element
or aspect of social reality might be defined as fundamental or
determinant, a position which receives expression in particular
in their respective criticisms of economistic tendencies in Marxist
analysis. Yet, however close and interesting such similarities
might seem, they do not make Foucault a 'neo-Weberian', for,
as I hope I have established, the differences remain more substantial.

In conclusion, the critical difference between the respective
analyses of Weber and Foucault might be summarised as follows.
The impulse behind Weber's work, explicitly articulated in
Comte's positive philosophy, and shared by all the celebrated
founding figures in sociology, has been described as 'to fashion
intellectual tools that would yield hindsights serviceable to
foresights: *savoir pour prevoir, prevoir pour pouvoir*' (Gerth
and Mills, 1970, p. 44). It is the very conjunction of 'pouvoir-
savoir', or complex of power-knowledge relationships, within
which the human sciences have emerged and been effective,
which constitutes the focus of Foucault's critical analyses.

ANOTHER CRITICAL THEORY

Although there are many interesting differences between the
various contributions to critical theory, for example between
the formulations to be found in the respective works of Adorno,
Horkheimer, Marcuse, and Habermas, there is a common underlying position, namely a criticism of instrumental reason or
rationality (cf. Jay, 1973; Held, 1980). It is the presence of
a critique of instrumental rationality at the very foundation of
critical theory which has prompted comparison with the work
of Foucault.

The general criticism articulated by the critical theorists is
that instrumental rationality has become the vehicle of oppression or domination of the human condition. In their view the

ascendancy of a particular form of reason, synonymous with the development of the mathematical and physical sciences, has made possible a technological mastery over the environment. One effect of the rise of instrumental rationality, itself subject to the logic and organisation of the capitalist mode of production, has been the generation of a process of reification which has produced an objectification of the world, the very process of disenchantment which had aroused Weber's fears. There are several formulations of this development in the work of the critical theorists (cf. Horkheimer, 1972, 1974; Wellmer, 1974; Habermas, 1971); however, they ultimately all reduce to a common criticism of the form of domination effected through a specific form of reason, instrumental rationality. As Horkheimer observed:

> Reason has become completely harnessed to the social process. Its operational value, its role in the domination of men and nature, has been made the sole criterion. (1974, p. 21)

A history of critical theory may be conceptualised in terms of the development of critiques of the forms of knowledge associated with the process of rationalisation and of the interrelated forms of domination and their respective repressive effects. The methodological and political dimensions of critical theory have as their object the constitution of a critical social analysis which embodies an interest in the achievement of an emancipation of the human condition from 'seemingly "natural" constraint' (cf. Habermas, 1972, p. 311). There is, in other words, an implicit distinction in the works of the critical theorists between, on the one hand, instrumental rationality, which is associated with technical control over the social and physical environment and with the exercise of political domination, and, on the other hand, a liberating rationality, a critical form of reasoning which promises the possibility of an emancipation of the human condition from the tyranny of domination. In other words, although the critical theorists have tended to share Weber's conception of rationalisation as a global historical process, they have simultaneously dissociated themselves from Weber's conclusions, by arguing that the form of rationality associated with capitalism is not synonymous with rationality as such, that there remains, in principle, the possibility of a liberating rationality or reason (cf. Marcuse, 1972).

In their analyses of rationality and domination the critical theorists have expressed an aversion to closed philosophical systems and have revealed a suspicion of Marxist politics. However, their respective criticisms of Marxist thought and its limitations, of Leninist forms of political organisation, and of the reality of socialist society (cf. Marcuse, 1971) do not signify a complete disaffection with Marxism; rather they are indicative of a concern to revitalise Marxist thought, of an interest in a regeneration of the critical dimension in Marxism. Whether the

work of the critical theorists ultimately remains compatible with
historical materialism will no doubt continue to be a matter of
controversy (cf. Slater, 1977; Held, 1980); however, it is in
my view indisputable that their respective analyses, frequently
drawing upon and incorporating elements of non-Marxist philosophy, have developed in relation to, and have attempted to
resolve, the central problems of Marxism.

The respective analyses of the critical theorists and of
Foucault may be situated in relation to the writings of Marx,
Nietzsche, and Weber. However, whereas the work of the critical
theorists may be regarded as broadly compatible with the
general terms of reference of historical materialist analysis, the
work of Foucault represents a qualitatively different mode of
analysis, the influence of Nietzsche exceeding that of Marx.
The critical theorists have continued, in principle, to broadly
align themselves with the political goals of Marxism, ergo the
achievement of socialism and liberty, whilst simultaneously
recognising the risks attached to Leninist theory and practice,
and thereby to Marxist political strategy in general, as well as
the problem of the apparent absence of any revolutionary
agency in Western capitalist (and, for that matter, state socialist) societies. However, the recognition of such difficulties
has not precipitated any fundamental shift in the location of
critical theory; its principal theoretical and political reference
has continued to be to historical materialism (cf. Frankel,
1974).

In contrast, Foucault's work has critical implications for the
very idea of socialism, socialist practices, and socialist politics,
in so far as its analytic focus on the emergence of 'the social'
has revealed that an acceleration, or an extension, of the process of socialisation, whether of economic or of other relations,
is not necessarily a progressive development; indeed, the
essence of Foucault's position is that such a development represents a further refinement in the deployment of technologies
of power (cf. Minson, 1980). Therefore, on this particular
issue, it is evident that Foucault's work is of a quite different
order to that of the critical theorists, for it constitutes a
critical interrogation, in contrast to a basically internal revi-
sion and reformulation, of the political rationality underlying
Marxism. At the risk of oversimplification we might conclude
that while the work of the critical theorists has remained very
much in the shadow of Marxism, the work of Foucault constitutes an attempt to develop a different form of critical analysis
on the basis of a reactivation and development of particular
themes derived from the writings of Nietzsche.

ON CRITIQUE

In my earlier discussion I referred to Foucault's derivation of
a conception of genealogical research and analysis from Nietz-

sche's work, to his rejection of global and systematising forms
of theory, and description of genealogy as a form of critique.
In conclusion I would like to return to the conception of critique
in Foucault's work.

It has been argued by Gordon (1979) that the interpretation
of Foucault's analyses of power and knowledge relations as a
form of ideology critique comparable to the work of the Frankfurt School is misleading, for whereas the critical theorists
have treated 'all dominant and socially ratified forms of knowledge as masks and instruments of oppression' (ibid., p. 28),
Foucault's analyses are situated beyond good and evil, in a
concern with the historical interconnections between relations
of power (positive and productive rather than repressive) and
knowledge. Therefore, Gordon has concluded, Foucault's conception of the relationship between power and knowledge is
the very antithesis of that to be found in the work of the critical theorists.

Although we may wish to endorse the view that Foucault's
conception and analysis of power-knowledge relations is not
equivalent, or reducible, to the conception which has informed
the work of the critical theorists, namely of a relationship
between knowledge and ideology, this in no way exhausts the
grounds of comparison between the respective positions. For
the concept of critique has at least two different meanings in
the work of the critical theorists, and whilst one of these
undoubtedly signifies a process of reflection on humanly produced illusions, distortions, and systems of constraint - what
might be described as 'critique of ideology' - another, deeper
sense, derived from the Enlightenment, is present in critical
theory, namely of 'critique as oppositional thinking, as an
activity of unveiling or debunking' (cf. Connerton, 1976,
pp. 16-17). It is this latter sense which I believe is implied
in Foucault's references to his work as a form of critique.

Foucault has described genealogy as research directed towards a resurrection of local, popular, and disqualified knowledges through the production of critical discourses. The function of such discourses is to interrupt the smooth passage of
'regimes of truth', to disrupt those forms of knowledge which
have assumed a self-evident quality, and to engender a state
of uncertainty in those responsible for servicing the network
of power-knowledge relations, for example 'the judges of
normality', teachers, doctors, social workers, etc. (cf. Foucault,
1977b, p. 304; 1981a, pp. 11-12). Therefore, at the very heart
of genealogical analysis, is the activity of critique, rather than,
for example, the provision of programmes, prophecies, or policies. As Foucault has observed:

> Critique doesn't have to be the premise of a deduction which
> concludes: this then is what needs to be done. It should be
> an instrument for those who fight, those who resist and
> refuse what is. Its use should be in processes of conflict

and confrontation, essays in refusal. It doesn't have to lay
down the law for law. It isn't a stage in a programming. It
is a challenge directed to what is. (1981a, p. 13)

It is this sense of critique which constitutes a common denominator between the work of Foucault and the critical theorists.

I do not intend to push the question of similarities between
the respective works of Foucault and the critical theorists any
further than an identification of the presence of a comparable
commitment to critique. Although critical theory emerged and
has developed in response to a growing awareness of the limits
and limitations of Marxism, it has remained broadly within the
Marxist tradition, analysing the consequences for Marxist
politics of the disappearance of a revolutionary agency, and
considering the implications for critical theorising of the likelihood that the moment at which a unification of theory and praxis
might have been realised has passed. Therefore the focus of
the work of the critical theorists has increasingly been on the
conditions of oppression and exploitation in late capitalist
societies.

As a consequence of their adoption of the master concepts of
historical materialism, the work of the critical theorists has
generally remained within the limits of the Marxist tradition
and has displayed comparable limitations. For example, their
observations on the disappearance of critical political forces
arise directly from an adoption of Marxist conceptions of power
and politics which are unable to encompass the multiplicity of
forms of resistance and opposition which, in turn, are not
reducible to, or exhausted by, the conception of a binary division of social forces into class terms. In other words it is not
that 'negative' or critical political forces have disappeared, but
that they do not necessarily take the form anticipated by the
political rationality of Marxism.

Although the work of Foucault may be situated in relation to
the limits and limitations of Marxism, its relationship to the
Marxist tradition is an external and generally critical one. The
objective of Foucault's analysis is not the construction or preservation of a particular 'truth' within theory, or a formulation
of the process by which theory might be realised in practice,
or an elevation of theory as the final refuge of resistance.
Rather, the objective has been an analysis of the interrelationship between the formation of domains and objects (e.g. madness, sexuality, etc.) and their articulation within discourse -
itself subject to rules and procedures of verification and falsi-
fication - and the effects of this complex relationship 'in the
real'. In brief, it is the 'politics of truth' with which Foucault
has been concerned: how we govern ourselves and others by
the production of truth, 'the establishment of domains in which
the practice of true and false can be made at once ordered and
pertinent' (cf. 1981a, pp. 8-9; 1980a, pp. 132-3).

If the work of Foucault reveals, to a degree, a comparable

general critical orientation towards some of the effects of technical control associated with an extension and development of rationalisation to that present in the Marxist tradition, in the work of the critical theorists, and to a lesser extent in Weber's work, it nevertheless remains ultimately distinctively different, in so far as rationalisation is conceived and studied neither as a uniformly global and homogeneous process nor as an entirely negative and repressive event, but is instead analysed in terms of the particular rationalities governing positive and productive social technologies of power, and the effects of the latter within ostensibly discrete fields of human experience (e.g. madness, illness, transgression of laws, sexuality). Finally, whereas within the Marxist tradition and in the work of the critical theorists there is the clear implication of a higher rationality, a liberating reason, which is to be nurtured by an intellectual vanguard, or a mandarin-like estate, whilst awaiting the emergence of a revolutionary subject capable of constructing a rational society, in Foucault's work there is no absolute 'value-of-reason'. The thrust of Foucault's work is not to subvert one notion of rationality, as capitalistic, instrumental, and technical, with another, 'higher' form which is socialist, intrinsically emancipatory, and enlightening, but to analyse rationalities, in particular how relations of power are rationalised.

The investment of the political rationality of socialism with absolute value has indirectly contributed to a further concealment of the social relations and practices through which the human condition has become increasingly subject to the exercise of particular forms of power. The cultivation of a detailed understanding of the various forms of power relations, associated rationalities and their effects is vital if a repetition of history, the replacement of discredited institutions and social practices with others which ultimately reveal comparable objectives and produce similar outcomes, is to be avoided. It is here, in analyses that attempt to reveal the complex processes and practices by which relations between people are regulated, governed, and rationalised, that the work of Foucault has made a significant contribution to radical theory and politics.

BIBLIOGRAPHY

Adorno, T.W. (1973), 'Negative Dialectics', New York, Seabury Press.
Althusser, L. (1969), 'For Marx', Harmondsworth, Penguin Books.
Althusser, L. (1971), 'Lenin and Philosophy and Other Essays', London,
  New Left Books.
Althusser, L. (1976), 'Essays in Self-Criticism', London, New Left Books.
Althusser, L. (1978a), The Crisis of Marxism, 'Marxism Today', vol. 22,
  no. 7.
Althusser, L. (1978b), What Must Change in the Party, 'New Left Review',
  no. 109.
Althusser, L., and Balibar, E. (1972), 'Reading Capital', London, New Left
  Books.
Altvater, E., and Kallscheuer, O. (1979), Socialist Politics and the 'Crisis of
  Marxism', in R. Miliband and J. Saville (eds), 'The Socialist Register 1979',
  London, Merlin Press.
Amnesty International (1975), 'Prisoners of Conscience in the USSR: Their
  Treatment and Conditions', London, Amnesty International Publications.
Anderson, P. (1976), 'Considerations on Western Marxism', London, New Left
  Books.
Anderson, P. (1980), 'Arguments within English Marxism', London, Verso
  Editions, New Left Books.
Bahro, R. (1978), 'The Alternative in Eastern Europe', London, New Left
  Books.
Berlinguer, E. (1982), 'After Poland', Nottingham, Spokesman Books.
Blackburn, R. (1977), Marxism: Theory of Proletarian Revolution, in
  R. Blackburn (ed.), 'Revolution and Class Struggle: A Reader in Marxist
  Politics', London, Fontana.
Bobbio, N. (1979a), Marxism and Socialism, 'Telos', no. 39.
Bobbio, N. (1979b), Gramsci and the Conception of Civil Society, in C. Mouffe,
  (ed.), 'Gramsci and Marxist Theory', London, Routledge & Kegan Paul.
Boffa, E. (1976), The Beginnings of Eurocommunism, 'EUROred', no. 5.
Brus, W., et. al., (1982), Outlook for the Socialist Economies, 'Marxism
  Today', vol. 26.
Callinicos, A. (1982), 'Is There a Future for Marxism?', London, Macmillan.
Carlo, C. (1980), The Crisis of Bureaucratic Collectivism, 'Telos', no. 43.
Castoriadis, C. (1977), The Diversionists, 'Telos', no. 33.
Claudin, F. (1978), 'Eurocommunism and Socialism', London, New Left Books.
Connerton, P. (ed.) (1976), 'Critical Sociology', Harmondsworth, Penguin
  Books.
Cutler, A; Hindess, B; Hirst, P; and Hussain, A. (1977), 'Marx's "Capital"
  and Capitalism Today', vol. 1, London, Routledge & Kegan Paul.
Cutler, A; Hindess, B; Hirst, P; and Hussain, A. (1978), 'Marx's "Capital"
  and Capitalism Today', vol. 2, London, Routledge & Kegan Paul.
Debray, R. (1977), Springtime Weepers, 'Telos', no. 33.
Debray, R. (1981), 'Teachers, Writers, Celebrities: The Intellectuals of
  Modern France', London, Verso Editions, New Left Books.
Deleuze, G. (1975), Ecrivain Non: Un Nouveau Cartographe, 'Critique',
  no. 343.
della Torre, P.F., et al. (1979), Editors' Conclusion, in della Torre et al.
  (eds) (1979).

della Torre, P.F., et al. (eds) (1979), 'Eurocommunism: Myth or Reality', Harmondsworth, Penguin Books.

Deutscher, T. (1976), Intellectual Opposition in the USSR, 'New Left Review', no. 96.

Dews, P. (1979), The 'Nouvelle Philosophie' and Foucault, 'Economy and Society', vol. 8, no. 2.

Dews, P. (1980), The 'New Philosophers' and the End of Leftism, 'Radical Philosophy', no. 24.

Donzelot, J. (1979), The Poverty of Political Culture, 'Ideology and Consciousness', no. 5.

Donzelot, J. (1980),'The Policing of Families: Welfare Versus the State', London, Hutchinson.

Durkheim, E. (1964), 'The Division of Labour in Society', New York, Free Press.

Engels, F. (1971), Preface to the English Edition of 1888 of 'The Manifesto of the Communist Party', in L. Feuer (ed.), 'Marx and Engels: Basic Writings on Politics and Philosophy', London, Fontana.

Feher, F. (1980), Eastern Europe in the Eighties, 'Telos', no. 45.

Feldbrugge, F.J.H. (1975), 'Samizdat and Political Dissent in the Soviet Union', Leyden, A.J. Sijthoff.

Feuer, L.S. (1971), 'Marx and Engels: Basic Writings on Politics and Philosophy', London, Fontana.

Fine, B. (1979), Struggles against Discipline: The Theory and Politics of Michel Foucault, 'Capital and Class', no. 9.

Fleischmann, E. (1964), De Weber à Nietzsche, 'European Journal of Sociology', vol. 5, no. 2.

Fletcher, R. (1974), 'The Crisis of Industrial Civilization: The Early Essays of August Comte', London, Heinemann.

Foucault, M. (1971), Orders of Discourse, 'Social Science Information', vol. 10, no. 2.

Foucault, M. (1973), 'The Order of Things: An Archaeology of the Human Sciences', New York, Vintage Books.

Foucault, M. (1977a), 'Language, Counter-Memory, Practice: Selected Essays and Interviews', ed. D.F. Bouchard, Oxford, Blackwell.

Foucault, M. (1977b), 'Discipline and Punish: The Birth of the Prison', London, Allen Lane, Penguin Press.

Foucault, M. (1977c), 'The Archaeology of Knowledge', London, Tavistock.

Foucault, M. (1978), Politics and the Study of Discourse, 'Ideology and Consciousness', no. 3.

Foucault, M. (1979a), 'The History of Sexuality: Volume 1 An Introduction', London, Allen Lane, Penguin Press.

Foucault, M. (1979b), Governmentality, 'Ideology and Consciousness', no. 6.

Foucault, M. (1980a), 'Power/Knowledge: Selected Interviews and Other Writings 1972-1977', ed. C. Gordon, Brighton, Harvester Press.

Foucault, M. (1980b), The History of Sexuality: Interview, 'Oxford Literary Review', vol. 4, no. 2.

Foucault, M. (1981a), Questions of Method: An Interview with Michel Foucault, 'Ideology and Consciousness', no. 8.

Foucault, M. (1981b), Omnes et Singulatim, in S.M. McMurrin (ed.), 'The Tanner Lectures on Human Values', vol. 2, Cambridge University Press.

Foucault, M. (1982), Afterword: The Subject and Power, in 'Michel Foucault: Beyond Structuralism and Hermeneutics', ed. H.L. Dreyfus and P. Rabinow, Brighton, Harvester Press.

Frankel, B. (1974), Habermas Talking: An Interview, 'Theory and Society', vol. 1, no. 1.

Gerth, H.H., and Wright Mills, C. (1970), Introduction: The Man and His Work, in Weber (1970).

Giddens, A. (1979), 'Central Problems in Social Theory: Action, Structure and Contradiction in Social Analysis', London, Macmillan.

Glucksmann, A. (1968), Strategy and Revolution in France 1968: An Introduction, 'New Left Review', no. 52.

Glucksmann, A. (1970), Action, in C. Posner (ed.), 'Reflections on the Revo-
lution in France: 1968', Harmondsworth, Penguin Books.
Glucksmann, A. (1977), An Interview with Andre Glucksmann, 'Telos', no. 33.
Glucksmann, A. (1980), 'The Master Thinkers', Brighton, Harvester Press.
Gordon, C. (1979), Other inquisitions, 'Ideology and Consciousness', no. 6.
Gordon, C. (1980), Afterword, in Foucault (1980a).
Gramsci, A. (1976), 'Selections from the Prison Notebooks', ed. Q. Hoare,
and G. Nowell Smith, London, Lawrence & Wishart.
Gramsci, A. (1977), 'Selections from Political Writings 1910-1920', ed.,
Q. Hoare, London, Lawrence & Wishart.
Habermas, J. (1971), 'Towards a Rational Society', London, Heinemann.
Habermas, J. (1972), 'Knowledge and Human Interests', London, Heinemann.
Habermas, J. (1974), 'Theory and Practice', London, Heinemann.
Hall, S. (1977), Rethinking the 'Base and Superstructure' Metaphor, in
J. Bloomfield (ed.), 'Class, Hegemony and Party', London, Lawrence &
Wishart.
Hall. S. (1980), Nicos Poulantzas: State, Power, Socialism, 'New Left Review',
no. 119.
Haynes, V., and Semyonova, O. (1979), 'Workers Against the Gulag: The
New Opposition in the Soviet Union', London, Pluto Press.
Held, D. (1980), 'Introduction to Critical Theory: Horkheimer to Habermas',
London, Hutchinson.
Hindess, B. (1977), The Concept of Class in Marxist Theory and Politics, in
'Class, Hegemony and Party', ed. J. Bloomfield, London, Lawrence &
Wishart.
Hindess, B., and Hirst, P.Q. (1977), 'Mode of Production and Social Formation:
An Auto-Critique of Pre-capitalist Modes of Production', London, Macmillan.
Hoffman, J. (1975), 'Marxism and the Theory of Praxis', London, Lawrence &
Wishart.
Holloway, J., and Picciotto, S. (eds) (1978), 'State and Capital: A Marxist
Debate', London, Edward Arnold.
Holubenko, M. (1975), The Soviet Working Class: Discontent and Opposition,
'Critique', no. 4.
Horkheimer, M. (1972), 'Critical Theory: Selected Essays', New York, Seabury
Press.
Horkheimer, M. (1974), 'Eclipse of Reason', New York, Seabury Press.
Horkheimer, M., and Adorno, T. (1973), 'The Dialectic of Enlightenment',
London, Allen Lane, Penguin Press.
Ingrao, P. (1979), 'Eurocommunism' and the Question of the State, 'EUROred',
no. 9.
Jay, M. (1973), 'The Dialectical Imagination: A History of the Frankfurt
School and the Institute of Social Research 1923-50', London, Heinemann.
Kolakowski, L. (1971), 'Marxism and Beyond: On Historical Understanding
and Individual Responsibility', London, Paladin.
Kolakowski, L. (1978), 'Main Currents of Marxism: Its Origins, Growth and
Dissolution', Oxford, Clarendon Press.
Laclau, E. (1977), 'Politics and Ideology in Marxist Theory', London, New
Left Books.
Laclau, E., and Mouffe, C. (1981), Socialist Strategy: Where Next?, 'Marxism
Today', vol. 25, no. 1.
Lea, J. (1979), Discipline and Capitalist Development, in B. Fine et al. (eds),
'Capitalism and the Rule of Law: From Deviancy Theory to Marxism', London,
Hutchinson.
Lecourt, D. (1975), 'Marxism and Epistemology: Bachelard, Canguilhem and
Foucault', London, New Left Books.
Lefort, C. (1978), Then and Now, 'Telos', no. 36.
Lenin, V.I. (1964), 'Collected Works', vol. 26, London, Lawrence & Wishart.
Lenin, V.I. (1965), 'Collected Works', vol. 28, London, Lawrence & Wishart.
Levi, A. (1979), Eurocommunism: Myth or Reality?, in P.F. della Torre et al.
(eds) (1979).
Lévy, B.-H. (1979), 'Barbarism with a Human Face', New York, Harper & Row.

McLellan, D. (1971), 'The Thought of Karl Marx', London, Macmillan.
Mandel, E. (1974), Solzhenitsyn, Stalinism and the October Revolution, 'New Left Review', no. 86.
Mao TseTung (1971), 'Selected Readings', Peking, Foreign Language Press.
Marcuse, H. (1969), 'Eros and Civilization', London, Sphere Books.
Marcuse, H. (1971), 'Soviet Marxism: A Critical Analysis', Harmondsworth, Penguin Books.
Marcuse, H. (1972), 'Negations: Essays in Critical Theory', Harmondsworth, Penguin Books.
Markovic, M. (1981), New Forms of Democracy and Socialism, 'Praxis International', vol. 1, no. 1.
Marx, K. (1973), 'The Revolutions of 1848', ed. D. Fernbach, Harmondsworth, Penguin Books.
Marx, K. (1976a), 'Capital', vol. 1, Harmondsworth, Penguin Books.
Marx, K. (1976b), 'Collected Works', vol. 5, London, Lawrence & Wishart.
Marx, K. (1977), 'Selected Writings', ed. D. McLellan, Oxford University Press.
Medvedev, R. (1974a), On Gulag Archipelago, 'New Left Review', no. 85.
Medvedev, R. (1974b), What Lies Ahead for Us, 'New Left Review', nos 87-8.
Medvedev, R. (ed.) (1977), 'The Samizdat Register 1', London, Merlin Press.
Melossi, D. (1979), Institutions of Social Control and Capitalist Organization of Work, in B. Fine et al. (eds), 'Capitalism and the Rule of Law', London, Hutchinson.
Mercer, C. (1980a), After Gramsci, 'Screen Education', no. 36.
Mercer, C. (1980b), Revolutions, Reforms or Reformulations? Marxist Discourse on Democracy, in A. Hunt (ed.), 'Marxism and Democracy', London, Lawrence & Wishart.
Miliband, R. (1977), 'Marxism and Politics', Oxford University Press.
Miller, J. (1978), Some Implications of Nietzsche's Thought for Marxism, 'Telos', no. 37.
Minson, J. (1980), Strategies for Socialists? Foucault's Conception of Power, 'Economy and Society', vol. 9, no. 1.
Mouffe, C. (1979), Hegemony and Ideology in Gramsci, in C. Mouffe (ed.), 'Gramsci and Marxist Theory', London, Routledge & Kegan Paul.
Nietzsche, F. (1968), 'The Will to Power', New York, Vintage Books.
Nietzsche, F. (1969), 'On the Genealogy of Morals', New York, Vintage Books.
Pasquino, P. (1978), Theatrum Politicum: The Genealogy of Capital - Police and the State of Prosperity, 'Ideology and Consciousness', no. 4.
Patton, P. (1979), Of Power and Prisons, in 'Michel Foucault: Power, Truth, Strategy', ed. M. Morris and P. Patton, Sydney, Feral Publications.
Posner, C. (ed.) (1970), 'Reflections on the Revolution in France: 1968', Harmondsworth, Penguin Books.
Poster, M. (1975), 'Existential Marxism in Postwar France: From Sartre to Althusser', Princeton University Press.
Poulantzas, N. (1973), 'Political Power and Social Classes', London, New Left Books.
Poulantzas, N. (1978), 'State, Power, Socialism', London, New Left Books.
Rancière, J. (1977), Reply to Lévy, 'Telos', no. 33.
Ryan, A. (1970), 'The Philosophy of the Social Sciences', London, Macmillan.
Saunders, G. (ed.) (1974), 'Samizdat: Voices of the Soviet Opposition', New York, Monad Press.
Sheridan, A. (1980), 'Michel Foucault: The Will to Truth', London, Tavistock.
Silnitsky, F., Silnitsky, L., and Reyman, K. (eds) (1979), 'Communism and Eastern Europe', Brighton, Harvester Press.
Slater, P. (1977), 'Origin and Significance of the Frankfurt School', London, Routledge & Kegan Paul.
Smart, B. (1982), Foucault, Sociology and the Problem of Human Agency, 'Theory and Society', vol. 11, no. 2.
Smart, B. (1983), Discipline and Social Regulation: On Foucault's Genealogical Analysis, in D. Garland and P. Young (eds), 'The Power to Punish', London, Heinemann.

Solzhenitsyn, A. (1978), 'The Gulag Archipelago', vol. 3, London, Fontana.
Solzhenitsyn, A. (1980), 'The Gulag Archipelago', vol. 1, London, Fontana.
Stedman Jones, G. (1973), Engels and the End of Classical German Philosophy, 'New Left Review', no. 79.
Taylor, G. (1980), The Marxist Inertia and the Labour Movement, 'Politics and Power', 1, London, Routledge & Kegan Paul.
Texier, J. (1979), Gramsci, Theoretician of the Superstructure, in Mouffe (1979).
Therborn, G. (1976), 'Science, Class and Society', London, New Left Books.
Thompson, E.P. (1967), Time, Work-Discipline, and Industrial Capitalism, 'Past and Present', no. 38.
Thompson, E.P. (1978), 'The Poverty of Theory and Other Essays', London, Merlin Press.
Time (1977), France's New Thinkers, 'Time', vol. 110, no. 10.
Valenta, J. (1980), Eurocommunism and the USSR, 'Political Quarterly', vol. 51, no. 2.
Weber, M. (1966), 'The Theory of Social and Economic Organisation', New York, Free Press.
Weber, M. (1968), 'Economy and Society', New York, Bedminster Press.
Weber, M. (1970), 'From Max Weber: Essays in Sociology', ed. H.H. Gerth and C. Wright Mills, London, Routledge & Kegan Paul.
Weber, M. (1976), 'The Protestant Ethic and the Spirit of Capitalism', London, Allen & Unwin.
Weil, B. (1981), Current Opposition in the Soviet Union, 'Praxis International', vol. 1, no. 1.
Wellmer, A. (1974), 'Critical Theory of Society', New York, Seabury Press.
Wildt, A. (1979), Totalitarian State Capitalism: On the Structure and Historical Function of Soviet-Type Societies, 'Telos', no. 41.
Williams, R. (1977), 'Marxism and Literature', Oxford University Press.
Williams, R. (1980), 'Problems in Materialism and Culture', London, Verso Editions, New Left Books.
Yaffe, D., and Bullock, P. (1975), Inflation, the Crisis and the Post-war Boom, 'Revolutionary Communist', nos 3-4.

INDEX